Czeolic

Text by Mike Ivory
Principal photographer: Richard Nebesky
Series Editor: Tony Halliday

Berlitz POCKET GUIDE
Czech Republic

First Edition 2007

PHOTOGRAPHY CREDITS
AKG-Images 17; Pete Bennett 24, 27, 30, 35, 89; Bridgeman 15, Corbis 22; Four Corners 61, 86; Glyn Genin 32, 39, 45, 88, 94, 101; Getty Images 21; Gavin Heller 28; Richard Nebesky 2–3, 6, 8, 11, 13, 33, 36, 40, 41, 43, 46, 49, 50, 51, 53, 54, 57, 62, 63, 65, 66–7, 69, 71, 73, 74, 76, 77, 79, 80, 81, 82, 85, 90, 93, 98, 103; Pictures Colour Library 97; Mark Read 9, 56, 58; Phil Wood 18
Cover picture: David Sanger Photography/Alamy

CONTACTING THE EDITORS
Every effort has been made to provide accurate information in this publication, but changes are inevitable. The publisher cannot be responsible for any resulting loss, inconvenience or injury. We would appreciate it if readers would call our attention to any errors or outdated information by contacting Berlitz Publishing, PO Box 7910, London SE1 1WE, England.
Fax: (44) 20 7403 0290
Email: berlitz@apaguide.co.uk
<www.berlitzpublishing.com>

Printed in Singapore by Insight Print Services (Pte) Ltd, 38 Joo Koon Road, Singapore 628990.
Tel: (65) 6865-1600. Fax: (65) 6861-6438

Berlitz Trademark Reg. U.S. Patent Office and other countries. Marca Registrada

Olomouc, once Moravia's capital, has the greatest number of listed buildings outside Prague (page 69)

Walkers head for Šumava National Park, known as the 'Green Roof of Europe' (page 53)

Telč, with its beautiful Renaissance and Baroque buildings (page 81)

TOP TEN ATTRACTIONS

Tour the wine villages of southern Moravia near the Slovak border (page 74)

Český Krumlov, on a bend in the River Vltava, is a medieval jewel of a town (page 51)

With a fine castle, handsome Old Town and lively Charles Bridge, Prague is not to be missed (page 25)

The ravines, rock formations and woodlands of Bohemian Switzerland (page 62) are popular with nature-lovers

Take the waters at the historic spa town of Karlovy Vary (page 55)

The Astronomical Clock, a feature of Prague's Old Town (page 33)

Explore Punkevní jeskyně cave by boat in the Moravian Karst (page 77)

CONTENTS

A ➤ in the text denotes a highly recommended sight

Fact Boxes

INTRODUCTION

In 2004, 15 years after the Velvet Revolution had freed it from Communism, the Czech Republic became a fully fledged member of the European Union. This marked the rightful return of the country to the heart of Europe, a place denied it for decades because of its location on the wrong side of the Iron Curtain. Even under Communism, Prague had attracted its fair share of foreign visitors; after 1989, their numbers increased enormously, making the city one of the world's most popular short-break destinations. The rest of the country has been less favoured, despite the existence of a number of hot spots such as the famous spa town of Karlovy Vary (Carlsbad) or the medieval jewel of Český Krumlov. Yet within its small compass, this little country has so much to offer. Its varied landscapes include bare mountains, glorious forested uplands, river gorges, remarkable rock formations and spectacular cave systems, but its greatest assets are man-made; its heritage of historic towns and fine buildings has few equals in Europe, and it is a treasure house of the work of artists of all kinds. The country's central location means it is easily accessible from abroad, while short distances and a well-developed transport infrastructure make it exceptionally easy to get around. Hotels and restaurants are of an increasingly high standard and offer excellent value, though Prague now matches other capital cities for prices.

The Country
The Czech Republic comprises the historic regions of Bohemia (in the west) and Moravia (in the east). It is the westernmost Slav country, pointing like an arrow into the territory of

Statue of John Nepomuk in Telč

its largest neighbour, Germany. To the south it borders Austria, to the north Poland, while to the east a new frontier has separated it since 1993 from Slovakia, its one-time partner in Czechoslovakia. Much of the frontier consists of mountains and wooded heights, forming what appear to be natural ramparts, albeit ones penetrated by numerous road and rail routes.

The most dramatic range, shared with Poland, is the Krkonoše or Giant Mountains, which include the country's highest point, Sněžka (1,602m/5,255ft). The weather at this altitude can be harsh at any time of the year, but the country as a whole has a temperate climate, though summers tend to be warmer and winters colder than in Western Europe. The whole of Bohemia is drained by the River Labe (or Elbe), which flows north into Germany. Moravia's great river is the Morava, whose basin opens southwards towards the lands bordering the Danube. Lacking a coastline, the Czech Republic makes the

Keystolovo Udoli, a typical village in northern Bohemia

most of its lakes, many of them formed by the damming of rivers. In southern Bohemia and Moravia whole landscapes are dominated by large and small ponds, the abode of the carp destined to become the country's favourite Christmas dinner.

Moravian costume

People

With 10.3 million inhabitants occupying its 78,864 sq km (30,449 sq miles), the Czech Republic is one of the most densely populated countries in Europe, with towns and villages scattered over most of its landscape. Over a tenth of its citizens live in the capital, while most of the rest reside in the small and medium-sized towns characteristic of the country. Larger cities include Brno, the capital of Moravia, with just under 400,000 inhabitants, and the industrial conurbation of Ostrava, with a population of around a third of a million.

The Czechs (including the Moravians) are a Slav people. Ruled by Austria for hundreds of years, they are considered by other, more romantically inclined Slavs to have acquired typically German traits like industriousness and efficiency, tempered by a healthy dose of cynicism. They don't expect much from authority, which they are more inclined to subvert or get round than confront head on. Private life is very important, with much attention given to the family and the home, as well as to the *chata*, the country cottage to which all town-dwellers aspire and to which they retreat every weekend.

The loss of Czech Jewry in the Holocaust and the postwar expulsion of the Germans made the country ethnically

Czech and Slovak are separate, but closely related languages, their differences akin to those distinguishing southern English from Lowland Scots. Before the break-up of Czechoslovakia, national radio and TV used both languages, but nowadays young people on either side of the new border are finding it more difficult to understand one another easily.

very homogenous. Today's most noticeable minority are the Gypsies, some of them well integrated, others living in piteous circumstances in virtual apartheid.

Together with Slovak and Polish, the Czech language belongs to the West Slavonic group. It has a complex grammar, and the number of accents over letters give the written language a formidable appearance. At least it is pronounced pretty much as it looks, though even some natives find it difficult to get their tongues round the unique 'ř' sound (as in Dvořák). Like other peoples whose language is not widely spoken, Czechs tend to be good or at least reasonable linguists. Once widely understood, German has tended to give way to English.

Architecture and the Arts

Few countries are as rich in well-preserved medieval towns, many of them founded by royal decree and laid out in well-planned fashion, frequently on a chequerboard pattern focused on a central square. However, the most glorious period of building came in the late 17th and 18th centuries, when Prague – but not just Prague – was endowed with splendid palaces and churches in Baroque style, designed by some of Central Europe's greatest architects and often built by craftsmen brought from Italy.

The Czech countryside has more castles than it can cope with. Many a medieval stronghold (*hrad* in Czech) occupyies a site seemingly chosen as much for its beauty as for its strategic value. In later centuries, an established aristocracy preferred to build itself a more luxurious rural residence in the form of a palace or country house (*zámek* in Czech). More recent times saw no diminution of architectural achievement. The country was one of the great centres of building in Art Nouveau style (here called *Secese* or Secession), and there was even a uniquely Czech attempt to translate the insights of Cubism into architecture, notably in Prague's Black Madonna Building. Inter-war Czechoslovakia led the way in architectural Modernism, though this gave way to the dreariness of much Communist-era building, its lowest point being the monotonous housing estates of high-rise, system-built apartments that disfigure the outskirts of cities and towns.

These movements also affected the other arts. While Alfons Mucha is famous internationally, many Czech artists of the late 19th and early 20th century were equally talented,

Český Šternberg

The popularity of brass band music has only recently started to wane. One of the world's great pop songs, the polka *Roll out the Barrel*, was written by a Czech bandmaster, Jaromir Vejvoda, though few of the Westerners able to hum or whistle it are aware of its original title, *Škoda lásky* ('The Pity of Love').

among them the aptly named Cubist Bohumil Kubišta, the abstract pioneer František Kupka, the Realist sculptor Otto Gutfreund, the Surrealist Toyen and the visionary Jan Zrzavy.

Crafts have traditionally flourished just as much as the arts. The skills of local glassmakers were legendary in such north Bohemian centres as Jablonec, and artistic and practical glassware still makes an excellent souvenir. Other tableware includes fine porcelain, long made in such places as Karlovy Vary.

'Co Čech, to musikant!' ('Scratch a Czech and find a musician!') runs the saying, and indeed Czechs have always been among the most musical of nations. Mozart found a far more cordial reception in Prague than in Vienna, notably in 1787 when the premiere of his *Don Giovanni* received a rapturous reception at the Estates Theatre. In the 19th century, Dvořák and Smetana put their country at the heart of musical Europe. The young Dvořák had honed his skills in one of the innumerable village bands, and Czech musicians provided the Austro-Hungarian army with most of its bandmasters, establishing a strong tradition of stirring brass band music. Under the Communists, rock and roll became a symbol of dissidence, its most notable practitioners being the Plastic People of the Universe.

The Czech Republic's rich cultural heritage enchants all who visit the country, especially if they travel beyond Prague, when it can be savoured against a background of smaller towns and villages and some of Europe's most harmonious and appealing landscapes.

A BRIEF HISTORY

More than most peoples, the Czechs are aware of the history that has moulded them and which continues to affect their present and influence their future. In its present form as an independent, ethnically homogenous, democratic republic, their country has existed for barely a decade; before that, as a little nation, they were more often than not subjected to interference and domination by larger and more powerful neighbours.

Arrival of the Czechs

In prehistoric times, most of the territory of what is now the Czech Republic was covered in dense woodland, with human settlement mainly confined to the low-lying valleys of the Labe (Elbe) and Morava rivers. The first recorded inhabitants of the region were Celtic tribes, known to the Romans as the Boii, the origin of the English terms for the country and its people (Bohemia/Bohemians). In the 1st century AD they were displaced by Germanic groups, who in their turn moved away, making room from the 6th century AD onwards for Slav tribes coming from the

Primeval forest once covered the land

The founding legend of the Přemyslid dynasty goes back to a vision experienced by a princess, Libuša, which led her to choose a ploughman, Přemysl, as her husband.

northeast. During the 9th century, the different tribes were briefly united in a realm centred on Moravia, later called the Great Moravian Empire. Christian influences came first from the west, then from the southeast in the persons of the monks Cyril and Methodius, brothers from Salonika who became known as the 'Apostles of the Slavs'.

Power eventually moved westwards to Bohemia, where the Czechs had consolidated their dominion over the other Slav tribes and founded a dynasty, the Přemyslids, who ruled until the 14th century. The 'Good King Wenceslas' of the English carol was a Přemyslid, but the greatest of the Přemyslid rulers was Ottakar II (1230–78), known as the 'King of Gold and Iron' for his prowess in war and the prosperity he brought the kingdom. Ottakar encouraged German merchants, miners and craftsmen to colonise the empty borderlands, populate new urban settlements and exploit Bohemia's abundant mineral resources. His ambitions were terminated when he was slain in battle by his Austrian rival for the imperial throne, Rudolf of Habsburg, the bearer of a family name destined to recur fatefully in the course of Czech history.

Great Emperor, Turbulent Priest

The Přemyslid dynasty was succeeded by the House of Luxembourg. The first Luxembourg ruler of Bohemia was King John, who despite being blind, fought with the French against the English at Crécy in 1346. His son, Charles, became Holy Roman Emperor as well as King of Bohemia. As Emperor Charles IV from 1355 he was responsible for one of the most glittering periods in the country's history; to make Prague worthy of the role of imperial capital, he began an unparalleled programme of civic improvement, pushing work forward on St Vitus' Cathedral, spanning the Vltava with the splendid stone bridge now named after him, and laying out Prague's New Town. Outside the city, the great castle of Karlštejn rose as a sacred repository for the crown jewels. At his death in 1378, Charles was succeeded by his incompetent son, Václav IV, chiefly remembered for ordering the murder of his queen's confessor, Canon John Nepomuk, who was later to become one of the country's favourite saints.

King Wenceslas, 16th-century panel from Nelahozeves Castle

Protestants and Catholics

A movement against the corruption and worldliness of the Church was led by Jan Hus, a humble priest from south Bohemia. Preaching in Czech from the pulpit in Prague's Bethlehem Chapel, Hus was a Protestant before Protestantism, and fell foul of the authorities. Executed as a heretic in 1415, he inspired others even more radical than himself. Known as Hussites, his followers became notorious, both as religious fanatics and as fierce fighters, disturbing the peace of much of Central Europe until their defeat at the Battle of Lipany in 1434.

By the start of the 16th century, the majority of the country's inhabitants had become Protestants. This did not prevent the election of a Catholic Habsburg, Ferdinand I, as king in 1526, though the choice soon showed itself ill-advised. Ferdinand was less interested in fair-minded governance of Bohemia than in consolidating Habsburg power in Central Europe and restoring Catholicism to its rightful place. Tensions rose under his rule and that of his successors, including Emperor Rudolf II, who succeeded to the throne in 1576. One of the most colourful rulers of Bohemia, the eccentric Rudolf showed himself more interested in the arts and sciences and their ability to unlock the mysteries of the universe than in suppressing dissent. His court in Prague attracted some of the finest minds in Europe, as well as a host of less savoury hangers-on, among them alchemists and soothsayers. Rudolf was deposed in 1611 by his brother Matthias, who set about reversing the religious and other concessions extracted earlier from his predecessor. Opposition grew among an increasingly alarmed Bohemian aristocracy; on 23 May 1618, a group of noblemen stormed into Prague Castle and ejected a pair of the emperor's officials from a window; this incident,

Defenestrated!

Cornered in Prague Castle by their angry Protestant adversaries on 23 May 1618, two terrified imperial officials begged for mercy, but their pleas went unheeded. Bundled to the window along with their unfortunate secretary, they were forced out, though one of them clung desperately to the sill until his knuckles were broken by a sharp blow from a dagger. Their descent into the moat far below should have killed them, but to everyone's surprise, they survived the fall, and succeeded in making their escape. According to the Catholic version of the event, they were miraculously borne up by the Virgin Mary; the possibly more realistic Protestant account describes how their fall was broken by the monstrous mound of rubbish that had accumulated in the moat.

The Defenestration of 1618 by Wenzel von Broznik (1889)

the Prague Defenestration, was the starting signal for the disastrous Thirty Years War. A new king, Frederick of the Palatinate, was elected, but in 1620 his Protestant army was routed by the imperial forces on a low hill just outside Prague. What became known as the Battle of White Mountain has gone down as one of the blackest days in Czech history; its aftermath was marked by the public execution of leading Protestants and the expulsion from the country of all those who refused to convert to Catholicism.

Darkness and Enlightenment

The period following the Battle of White Mountain was characterised by later historians as the 'Darkness', a time when Czechs were a suppressed majority in their own land, their elite either dead or in exile, their language downgraded, and their favoured religion forbidden. Much of this was true. Confiscated Protestant estates were sold at knock-down prices to

Habsburg supporters, many of them of foreign, particularly German, origin. German became the language of polite society, and Czech was eventually spoken only by peasants and the urban poor. Jesuits and other religious orders strove to eliminate the last sparks of Protestantism. However, not all was gloom. Once the country had recovered from the decades of war, a building boom beautified cities and countryside with the glories of Baroque art and architecture.

National Awakening

In the 18th century Habsburg rule became more enlightened, notably in the reign of Emperor Joseph II (1780–90). His educational reforms produced a generation of literate Czechs, who became increasingly aware of their past history and their present subjugation. In the early 19th century a new intellectual elite emerged, codifying the Czech language, reviving its

Prague's National Theatre, symbol of Czech national pride

literature and agitating for Czech rights within the Empire. During the course of the Industrial Revolution, Bohemia and Moravia emerged as Austria's industrial powerhouse. Small-scale industries sprang up in the borderlands, while Ostrava expanded on coal and iron and Brno became known as the 'Austrian Manchester' thanks to its thriving textile work-shops. German dominance of the towns diminished as fac-tories drew in Czech workers from the countryside. By the end of the century, Prague, which Emperor Franz Josef had described earlier as looking 'every bit a German city', was completely in the hands of the Czechs; street signs in German had disappeared, and bombastic buildings like the National Museum and National Theatre expressed an ever more confident Czech nationalism.

The First Republic

In World War I, Czechs found themselves fighting alongside Germans against their Russian fellow-Slavs. While most served their emperor loyally, many deserted, and along with prisoners of war, formed Czechoslovak legions to fight with the Allies in the hope of gaining independence from Austria. They supplied useful backing for exiled politicians striving for the same aim, notably Professor Tomáš Garrigue Masaryk and his assistant Eduard Beneš.

As the Habsburg Empire collapsed in late 1918, Czechs and Slovaks proclaimed the new state of Czechoslovakia, consist-ing of Bohemia, Moravia, a slice of Silesia, Slovakia, and Ruthenia, an easternmost appendix adjoining the Soviet Union. In many ways a model state, this First Czechoslovak Republic suffered from structural faults which were to prove fatal two decades later. A self-declared 'state of Czechs and Slovaks', it contained sizeable minorities, with Germans actu-ally outnumbering Slovaks. Promises of autonomy made to Slovakia and Ruthenia were never honoured. Problems were

Tomáš Masaryk was elected the first president of Czechoslovakia in 1918. With a Moravian mother, a Slovak father, educated in German, and with an impeccably liberal outlook, he seemed destined to lead his country with success. His middle name of Garrigue was the surname of his American wife, and reflected his Western orientation.

masked by prosperity in the 1920s, and the new republic had many achievements to its credit: a progressive social policy, a functioning democracy (rare in Central Europe), an explosion of cultural activity and a flourishing economy. But in the 1930s, the Great Depression wrecked the economy, while the lure of the Third Reich proved irresistible to Sudeten Germans – as the members of the country's Germanic minority now called themselves. Encouraged by Hitler, they made demands which were impossible to fulfil within the framework of democratic Czechoslovakia. At Munich, in September 1938, Britain and France supinely agreed to cede the Sudetenland to Nazi Germany, depriving the country of much of its industry and the whole of its formidable line of fortifications.

The Protektorat

In March 1939, after persuading Slovak nationalists to secede and form an ostensibly independent, near-Fascist 'Slovak State', Hitler incorporated the remainder of the country into Greater Germany as the 'Protectorate of Bohemia-Moravia' under the leaderhip of SS General Reinhard Heydrich. In exile, President Beneš laboured to gain the approval of the Allies for a reconstituted Czechoslovakia. The vicious Nazi reaction to Heydrich's assassination (see page 40) filled Czech hearts with hate, ensuring universal support for the planned post-war expulsion of the country's 3 million Germans. As the war drew to an end, most of the country was liberated by the Red Army.

New Darkness

Beneš's enjoyment of his achievement in reviving his country was short-lived. The unscrupulous Communists formed the most powerful party, overseeing the expulsion of the Germans, the expropriation of landed estates and the nationalisation of important industries. In February 1948, they engineered a coup which gave them complete control. Beneš resigned as president in favour of the Communist leader, Klement Gottwald, and the country's most popular politician, Masaryk's son Jan, fell to his death in another, still unexplained defenestration. Thousands fled the country, thousands more were imprisoned or sent to the country's uranium mines, while others were executed after Stalinist-style show trials. The short-lived 'Prague Spring' of 1968 saw an attempt by reform Communists led by the Slovak Alexander Dubček to transform the system and create a 'Socialism with a human face'. This failed, crushed by the Soviet tanks which overran the country in August. For the next two decades, reinstated hardline Communists ruled the roost, buying off the populace by filling the shop shelves with consumer goods, albeit of poor quality. The few dissidents, among them playwright Václav Havel, suffered routine harassment and persecution.

Students distribute literature during the 'Prague Spring'

Czech and Slovak Republics

In November 1989, a bloodily broken-up student demonstration provoked mass protests, which the regime proved powerless to resist. The so-called Velvet Revolution saw Václav Havel elected as president, an office he was to hold for 13 years, though the name of the country he presided over was to change. While successive governments struggled with the awesome problems of converting the Communist system into a free-market economy, Havel fought for the survival of the country whose freedom he had suffered for. In vain: in 1992, the Czech prime minister Václav Klaus and nationalist Slovak leader Vladimir Mečiar decided that the only way to settle their differences was for Czechoslovakia to be divided. Avoiding the referendum that would almost certainly have put paid to their plans, they engineered the 'Velvet Divorce', the creation of separate Czech and Slovak Republics.

The disappointed Havel submitted himself to re-election as president of his now diminished country, finally being replaced by Klaus in 2003. Despite setbacks, the Czech Republic has steadily integrated itself into the political and economic systems of the West. Membership of NATO came in 1999, and in 2004 the country joined the European Union. Two years previously, in August 2002, a flood had devastated towns and villages along the valley of the Vltava, including Prague. Many thought it would take decades for the country to recover, but the swift and competent way in which the disaster was tackled boded well for the future of this nation.

Václav Havel

Historical Landmarks

c. AD **500** Arrival of the Slavs.

c. **890** Prince Bořivoj of the Přemyslid dynasty builds Prague Castle.

c. **935** Assassination of 'Good King' Wenceslas by his brother.

1253–78 King Ottakar II extends the Bohemian kingdom over much of Central Europe and as far south as the Adriatic.

1346–78 Reign of Charles IV. Prague is capital of Holy Roman Empire.

1398–1415 Jan Hus preaches Church reform and is burnt at the stake.

1526 The crown of Bohemia passes to the Habsburg dynasty.

1576 Emperor Rudolf II makes Prague a seat of Renaissance art.

1618 Prague Defenestration marks the start of the Thirty Years War.

1620 Protestant army defeated at the Battle of White Mountain.

Late 17th/18th century Town and country beautified by construction of Baroque churches, palaces and castles. German is the language of polite society.

1780 Reformist Emperor Joseph II abolishes serfdom and awards Jews civic rights.

1805 Napoleon defeats a combined Austrian and Russian army at the Battle of Austerlitz, fought near Brno.

1848 The 'Year of Revolutions'. A nationalist uprising in Prague is crushed by Austrian forces.

1866 The Austrian army is defeated by the Prussians at the Battle of Königgrätz (Hradec Králové).

1918 Collapse of Austria-Hungary and foundation of Czechoslovakia.

1938–9 Czechoslovakia is occupied by Nazi Germany.

1945 Liberation of western Bohemia by US forces and the rest of the country by the Red Army.

1948 Communist coup d'état.

1968 'Prague Spring' reformists put down by Warsaw Pact forces.

1989 'Velvet Revolution' overthrows Communist regime.

1993 Czechoslovakia divided into Czech and Slovak republics.

1999 Czech Republic joins NATO.

2004 Czech Republic becomes part of the European Union.

WHERE TO GO

Thanks to the relatively small size of the country, its excellent road network, good public transport and well organised group excursions, it is quite possible to use Prague as a base and visit many of the Czech Republic's major attractions in the course of a day trip. However, it is far more rewarding to overnight in a variety of places, ideally choosing somewhere to stay in each of the regions described in the following text. Be sure to include examples of all the country's riches in your itinerary, not just historic towns and villages, but also castles and country houses and the amazing variety of landscapes, many of them protected as national parks and nature reserves. Such an arrangement is perfectly possible using trains and buses, and has the advantage of bringing you into close contact with local life. But if time is short, car hire is easily arranged, and having your own vehicle gives flexibility and the possibility of visiting remoter places.

PRAGUE

For most of their history, Prague's four historic districts were independent towns, and they have retained their distinctive identity to this day. On a rock spur overlooking a bend in the broad River Vltava, hilltop **Hradčany** is the smallest. Here is Prague Castle, a little city in itself, with palaces, churches, galleries and other buildings grouped along cobbled lanes and around spacious courtyards. Spreading over the plateau beyond is a tranquil quarter of quiet streets and more palaces, reaching to the Strahov Monastery which guards the western approaches to the city. From here, the woods and orchards of Petřín Hill slope down to the **Malá Strana (Lesser Town)**.

Tram in Prague's Lesser Town

Squeezed between the hillside, the river and the castle ramparts, this is Prague's most intimate district, a little paradise of palaces and hidden gardens, centred on the sublime Church of St Nicholas. From Malá Strana, the Charles Bridge spans the Vltava to the **Staré Město (Old Town)**, whose labyrinth of narrow streets and lanes is centred on Old Town Square, the city's ancient commercial heart. Close by is the Josefov, the former ghetto, with its synagogues and Old Jewish Cemetery. Beyond the boulevards laid out along the line of the demolished city walls, the **Nové Město (New Town)** is new in name only, having been laid out in the 14th century by Emperor Charles IV. This is where modern Prague's heart beats most strongly, especially on tree-lined Wenceslas Square.

Beyond the historic centre, the suburbs offer many attractions, among them museums of outstanding interest, the city's second citadel, Vyšehrad, and, on the banks of the Vltava downstream, the palace of Troja, Prague's Versailles.

Hradčany

The rocky eminence on which Prague Castle stands was originally fortified in the 9th century by Prince Bořivoj, the founder of Bohemia's first royal dynasty. His Slav stronghold was strengthened and extended over the centuries, becoming the symbolic heart of the nation, its palace and cathedral the seats of princely and ecclesiastical power. In more recent times the residence of the president, since the end of Communism it has opened itself up ever more to the public, with enough galleries, gardens and splendid interiors to keep weekend visitors busy for the whole of their stay.

Prague Castle

Of the various approaches to **Pražský hrad** (Prague Castle; outside areas: open Apr–Oct daily 5am–midnight, Nov–Mar daily 6am–11pm; free; interiors: open Apr–Oct daily 9am–

View of the castle from the river

5pm, Nov–Mar daily 9am–4pm; various admission fees), the most imposing is from the west, past blue-uniformed sentries and a pair of battling stone giants, across the First Courtyard and through a Renaissance gateway into the Second Courtyard with its Baroque fountain. From here, another gateway leads across the deep ravine of the Stag Moat to the **Královská zahrada** (Royal Garden; open Apr–Oct daily 10am–6pm; free); at its far end stands the lovely mid-16th-century **Belvedere** or Summer Palace, one of the first Renaissance buildings in Central Europe. Back in the castle precinct, the Third Courtyard is dominated by the glorious Gothic **sv. Vít** (St Vitus' Cathedral). The cathedral nave was only completed in the 19th century, with much of its intensely colourful stained glass added in the 20th. One of the most striking windows is by Alfons Mucha. In style, the nave matches the chancel, begun on the orders of Emperor Charles IV by Matthew of Arras in 1344 and continued by Peter Parler and other members of his architectural dynasty. Access to this part of the cathedral, with its array of fabulous funerary monuments, its crypt and its jewel-like Wenceslas Chapel, is by ticket (open Apr–Oct Mon– Sat 9am–5pm, Sun noon–5pm, Nov–Mar Mon–Sat 9am–4pm, Sun noon–4pm; admission fee). The reward for making the long climb to the top of the cathedral tower is a superb view.

The Third Courtyard also gives access to the **Starý královský palác** (Old Royal Palace), the centrepiece of which is Vladislav Hall. With its Renaissance windows and writhing Late Gothic vaulting, this glorious ceremonial space is large enough to have been the scene of tournaments, with participants galloping up the Riders' Staircase at one end of the hall. Opening off it is the suite of rooms from which Catholic councillors were ejected in the Prague Defenestration of 1618.

The castle precinct's second great church is **sv. Jiří** (St George's Basilica), an austere Romanesque structure with

'Alchemists' cottages' in Golden Lane

twin towers and a blood-red Baroque façade. The adjacent **Jiřský klášter** (St George's Convent; open Tues–Sun 10am–6pm; admission fee) is the home of the National Gallery's superlative collection of Renaissance and Baroque painting and sculpture. Easily overlooked, this offers the chance to see works from a time when Prague was one of Europe's great centres of artistic activity. By contrast, one of the castle's most popular attractions is **Zlatá ulička** (Golden Lane; admission fee payable at castle information centre), the picturesque alleyway with its range of brightly painted 'alchemists' cottages'. An escape from the crowds is offered in the less constricted surroundings of the beautifully landscaped gardens atop the castle's southern ramparts.

To Strahov Monastery

Some of Prague's finest palaces line Hradčanské náměstí, the elongated square sloping gently uphill from the castle. None of them is more ostentatious than the sgraffitoed **Schwarzenberský palác**, undergoing reconstruction. (The decorative plasterwork known as sgraffito is everywhere to be seen in Prague. It is made by scraping off an upper layer of plaster to reveal the contrasting layer beneath.) In complete contrast, the **Šternberský palác** (open Tues–Sun 10am–6pm; admission fee) hides itself down an alleyway. It is the home of the National Gallery's holdings of European Old Master paintings.

From the square, lanes wind westwards along **Nový svšt** (New World), a quiet, village-like quarter once lived in by castle servants. Two very different edifices confront each other across Loretánské náměstí/Loretto Square. The home of the Foreign Office, the late 17th-century **Černínský palác** (Czernín Palace) is a vast structure that bankrupted the aristocratic family who built it. Opposite, the **Loreta** (Loretto; open Tues– Sun 9am–12.15pm, 1pm–4.30pm; admission fee) is a gorgeous Baroque confection of a building, erected

St Nicholas' Church in the Lesser Town

around the Santa Casa, a replica of the home of the Virgin Mary in the Holy Land. The precinct is surrounded by a cloister, and there is a little church with particularly sumptuous decoration, an equally sumptuous treasury, and a carillon that draws onlookers every hour. **Strahovský klášter** (Strahov Monastery; open daily 9am–noon, 1–5pm; admission fee) occupies a strategic site at the top of Petřín Hill, commanding views over the whole city. Its main attraction is its pair of libraries, the Theological and Philosophical Halls, with priceless books, maps and antique globes housed in interiors of great magnificence.

Malá Strana (Lesser Town)

The epicentre of the Lesser Town is the stupendous **sv. Mikuláš** (St Nicholas' Church; open Mar–Oct daily 9am–5pm, Nov–Feb daily 9am–4pm; admission fee), the country's greatest Baroque place of worship. Built to celebrate the triumph of the Counter-Reformation and to propagate the teachings of the Jesuits, it was begun in 1673 and worked on by the Dientzenhofer dynasty of architects. Its great dome can be seen from all over the city, while its interior is of unrivalled sumptuousness. From Malostranské náměstí (Malá Strana Square), with its busy tram stop, streets lead out to the district's other sights. To the north is the biggest of all Prague's palaces, the **Valdštejnský palace** (Wallenstein Palace; open Sat–Sun 10am–5pm; free). Now the home of the Senate, the palace was built by warlord Albrecht von Wallenstein in the 1620s. His walled formal garden (open Apr–Oct daily 10am–6pm; free) makes a magical setting for summer concerts. Of the streets climbing up towards the castle and Petřín Hill, **Nerudova** is the steepest and prettiest. It is lined with the occasional palace and with numerous lovely town houses, many of them with the charming pictorial house signs ('The Three Little Fiddles', 'The Red Lamb') once so characteristic of Prague. **Tržiště** (Market Street) is graced by the well-guarded US Embassy, housed in the Schönbornský palác. Further uphill, the German Embassy occupies the even grander Lobkovický palác (Lobkowicz Palace) in **Vlašská** (Italian Street), named after the immigrant artists and craftsmen largely responsible for Prague's Baroque beautification.

Leading south from the square, Karmelitská passes the city's most important place of pilgrimage, the church of **Panna Marie Vitězná** (Our Lady of Victories; open Mon–Sat 8.30am–7pm, Sun 8.30am–8pm; free). The church has the tiny 'Bambino di Praga', a statue of the infant Jesus, which has a huge cult following, particularly in Latin America. On the opposite side of the street, the new **České muzeum hudby** (Czech Music Museum; open Mon, Wed–Sun 10am–6pm; admission fee) does more than justice to this most musical of nations. Idyllic little streets and lanes lead from here towards the parkland of **Kampa** island, separated from the rest of Malá Strana by the millstream known as the Čertovká (Devil's Brook). One of the island's mills has been imaginatively rebuilt and houses the **Museum Kampa** (open daily 10am–6pm; admission fee; free Mon), with an immaculately presented collection of modern Czech and international art.

The Charles Bridge

Charles Bridge

For centuries the only bridge to span the Vltava, **Karlův most** (Charles Bridge) was never just a river crossing, but also a place of commerce, celebration and punishment. Begun in 1357 by Charles IV, it was enhanced in the late 17th and early 18th century by the addition of an array of statuary. Pride of place is occupied by the figure of St John Nepomuk, the patron saint of bridges *(see below)*. The bridge is guarded by chisel-roofed towers at either end; both can be climbed.

Patron Saint of Bridges

The most popular statue on Charles Bridge is probably the one of St John Nepomuk, Vicar General of St Vitus' Cathedral. For good luck, passers-by touch the panel on the base of the statue which shows the unfortunate cleric being thrown into the Vltava and left to drown. This event really took place, in March 1393, and it is said that Nepomuk suffered his dreadful fate for refusing to reveal the secrets of the queen's confessional to her jealous husband, the unstable King Wenceslas IV. As his body bobbed around in the icy waters, refusing to sink, a miraculous quintet of stars appeared to dance above him. Much later, in 1729, when the Counter-Reformation was in full swing and the Catholic Church needed a new saint to help erase the memory of radical Jan Hus, Nepomuk was canonised, and, as patron saint of bridges, his statue guards river crossings all over Central Europe.

Staré Město (Old Town)

Contained within the great bend of the Vltava, the Old Town was traditionally the place of tradespeople and artisans, the mercantile counterweight to Hradčany, the domain of Church and court. Nowadays its maze of cobbled streets, little squares, covered passageways and courtyards is home to countless small shops, restaurants and cafés. At its centre is **Staroměstské náměstí (Old Town Square)**, a picturesquely irregular space pulsing with life day and night. The principal landmark is the **Staroměstská radnice** (Old Town Hall; open Apr–Oct daily 9am–6pm, Mon from 11am, Nov–Mar daily 9am–5pm, Mon from 11am; admission fee), with ceremonial interiors and a tall tower. However the main attraction here is the **Orloj (Astronomical Clock)**, its medieval mechanism setting in motion the hourly parade of traditional figures: Death, Saviour and Apostles, Turk and Jew, Vice and Virtue. Peering over the arcaded buildings on the far side of the square are the dark and spiky towers of the **Týn Church**, while prominent buildings in the square itself include the city's second church dedicated to St Nicholas and the graceful **Palác Kinských** (Kinsky Palace; open Tues–Sun 10am–6pm; admission fee), home of the National Gallery's collec-

The Astronomical Clock

tion of Czech landscape painting. Nearby is the extraordinary 1915 monument to Jan Hus, the most ambitious work of the Art Nouveau sculptor Ladislav Šaloun.

The Ghetto

A century ago, the broad boulevard of **Pařížská** was bulldozed through the delapidated houses of the **Josefov**, the ghetto which had been the home of Prague's Jews for centuries. Spared from redevelopment were the district's synagogues, some of which are now museums. Foremost among them, and still in use, is the 13th-century **Staronová synagoga** (Old-New Synagogue; open Apr–Oct Sun–Thur 9.30am–5pm, Fri 9.30am–2pm, Nov–Mar Sun–Fri 9.30am–6pm; admission fee), with its high gables and atmospheric interior. At the turn of the 16th and 17th century, its most famous rabbi was Judah Loew ben Bazalel, creator of the Golem *(see below)*.

Close by is the **Starý židovský hřbitov** (Old Jewish Cemetery; open summer Sun–Fri 9am–6pm, winter Sun–Fri 9am–

The Golem

The giant man of clay called the Golem is Prague's equivalent of the Frankenstein monster. He is supposed to have been fashioned out of mud from the riverside by learned Rabbi Loew (c.1520–1609), master of many an arcane mystery. Obedient at first, the Golem performs his allotted tasks, but runs amok when the rabbi forgets to renew the charm that keeps him under control. Eventually he is overcome, and a spell reduces him once more to mud. His remains are shovelled up and stored among the rafters in the attic of the Old-New Synagogue, where they have been ever since. Woe betide anyone who has the temerity to disturb them! The most enduring image of the Golem is the one in the film of the same name, a silent-screen classic of the early cinema by the German director Paul Wegener.

4.30pm; admission fee), with its thousands of tumbledown tombstones crowded together in the dappled shade of trees.

Royal Way

Old Town Square lies on the Royal Way, the route taken by coronation processions on their way to the cathedral. The Way starts at the **Obecní dům** (Municipal House) of 1911, a glittering Art Nouveau building to which most of the leading artists and decorators of the day con-

The Old-New Synagogue

tributed, then passes the landmark **Prašá brána** (Powder Tower) and the **Dům u Černé Matky Boží** (Black Madonna Building), the finest example of architectural Cubism, that uniquely Czech phenomenon. Off the Way to the south is the **Stavovské divadlo** (Estates Theatre), where the premiere of Mozart's *Don Giovanni* was ecstatically received in 1787. Beyond Old Town Square, the Way follows an intricate and always thronged route to the riverside and Charles Bridge. To the south is the rebuilt **Betlémské kaple** (Bethlehem Chapel), from the pulpit of which Jan Hus preached.

In the north of the Old Town are two of the city's most important museums. The UPM (Decorative Arts Museum; open Tues 10am–7pm, Wed–Sun 10am–6pm; admission fee) displays a world-class array of arts and crafts, such as glass and porcelain for which Bohemia has always been famous, while the **Anežský klášter** (St Agnes' Convent; open Tues–Sun 10am–6pm; admission fee) houses the National Gallery's collections of medieval painting and sculpture.

Nové Město (New Town)

Emperor Charles IV's plan for the New Town has stood the test of time. It was conceived on such generous lines that it was able to accommodate Prague's growth well into the 19th century, and it is still the city's commercial heart. It was laid out around three main squares. Bustling **Václavské náměstí** ◄ (Wenceslas Square) is the most famous of the trio, and rightly so. Less of a square and more of a grand tree-lined boulevard, it rises gently towards the statue of Wenceslas on his steed and the great bulk of the **Narodní muzeum** (National Museum; open May–Sept daily 10am–6pm, Oct–Apr daily 9am–5pm; admission fee), with its rather dusty, mostly scientific collections. From the lower end of the square, **Národní třída** (National Avenue) leads west to the river and the **Národní divadlo** (National Theatre), built in 1881.

King Wenceslas presides over his square

The New Town has its share of the city's museums and other places of interest. Art-lovers may well wish to visit the **Muchovo Muzeum** (Mucha Museum; open Mar– Dec daily 10am–6pm, Jan–Feb daily 10am–5pm; admission fee), where justice is done to this internationally renowned Art Nouveau artist. Close to the most spacious of the New Town squares, park-like **Karlovo náměstí** (Charles Square), is

sv. Cyril a Metoděj (Church of Saints Cyril and Methodius), the church where in June 1942 the parachutist assassins of Reichsprotektor Heydrich made their last stand.

Suburban Prague

During the Middle Ages, the well-fortified **Vyšehrad** rock dominating the Vltava just to the south of the centre was used for a while by the country's rulers as an alternative citadel to Hradčany. In the 19th century, Vyšehrad became a focus of nationalist feeling and was chosen as the site of the national cemetery. Here the country's great and good have been laid to rest, among them Dvořák and Smetana. On the far bank of the Vltava, in what is now the industrial suburb of Smíchov, Mozart composed the final notes of *Don Giovanni* while staying at the **Bertramka** (open Apr–Oct daily 9.30am–6pm, Nov–Mar daily 9.30am–5pm; admission fee).

Betrayed by one of their number, and besieged by the Gestapo and SS, the parachutists hiding in the crypt of the Church of Saints Cyril and Methodius fought back bravely. Their resistance came to an end only when the Prague fire brigade was forced to fill the crypt with water. Rather than surrender, the survivors used their last bullets on themselves.

Two museums in the northern suburb of Holešovice merit attention. The **Národní technické muzeum** (National Technical Museum), currently being reconstructed, has a fine array of cars, trains and planes, while the **Veletržní palác** (Trades Fair Palace; open Tues–Sun 10am–6pm; admission fee) houses the national collections of 19th-, 20th- and 21st-century art. In more rustic surroundings, close to the zoo, **Trojský zámek** (Troja Palace; open Apr–Oct Tues–Sun 10am–6pm; Nov–Mar Sat–Sun 10am–5pm; admission fee) is one of the greatest Baroque palaces in the country. A restored formal garden and superb sculpted staircase complement the lavish interiors.

CENTRAL BOHEMIA

Few capital cities are as privileged as Prague in terms of real countryside within easy reach. 'Bohemia's Woods and Fields', celebrated in Smetana's symphonic poem *Má vlast*, begin as soon as the city's high-rise suburbs are left behind. The valleys cut by the Vltava and its tributaries are home to some wonderful architectural jewels, from medieval fortresses like Charles IV's Karlštejn to Renaissance treasure houses like Nelahozeves or the richly furnished stronghold of Archduke Franz Ferdinand at Konopiště. A favourite excursion from Prague is to the medieval city of Kutná Hora, its wealth of monuments built from the proceeds of its silver mines. Other towns like Litoměřice and wine-growing Mělník offer further scenic delights, while the ghetto city of Terezín and the memorial village of Lidice are chilling reminders of the horrors of mid-20th-century history.

Karlštejn and Křivoklát

Rising high above the treetops of the winding valley of the River Berounka like a medieval vision come true, the castle of **Karlštejn** is one of the great sights of Bohemia, drawing crowds of visitors throughout the year. It was begun by Emperor Charles IV in 1348 as a spiritual retreat and repository for the crown jewels and the sacred relics he collected. The castle's present appearance is partly the result of overzealous rebuilding in the 19th century.

An alternative to the long walk uphill from the village at the foot of the castle is to ride in one of the horse-drawn carriages. From here there is a choice of two tours. Tour I (Tues–Sun, July–Aug 9am–6pm, May–June, Sept 9am–5pm, Apr, Oct 9am–4pm, early Mar, late Dec, early Jan 9am–3pm; admission fee) takes in the imperial palace and the Marian tower which is Karlštejn's dominant feature. Tour II (Tues–Sun, June–Oct,

The magnificent castle of Karlštejn, built as a retreat for Charles IV

hours as above; admission fee, advance booking essential, tel: 274 008 154, email: <reservace@stc.npu.cz>) reveals the castle's sacred heart, a sequence of gorgeously decorated interiors. They include the Chapel of St Catherine, with wall-paintings set in a matrix of semi-precious stones, and the Chapel of the Holy Cross, with a starry vault and a stunning series of portraits by court painter Master Theodoric.

While Karlštejn is a short train ride from Prague, the medieval castle at **Křivoklát** (open May–Aug Tues–Sun 9am–5pm, Apr, Sept Tues–Sun 9am–4pm, Mar, Oct Tues–Sun 9am–3pm, Nov–mid-Dec Sat–Sun 9am–3pm; admission fee) lies much deeper in the countryside, high above a tributary of the Berounka. Surrounded by vast forests, it originated as a royal hunting lodge in the 12th century. Rebuilt and extended, it continued its role as a royal residence and is everything a feudal fortress should be, with sturdy walls and towers frowning down from a commanding height, and authentic medieval interiors.

Lidice, where a village once stood

Lidice

Following the assassination of Reichsprotektor Heydrich on 27 May 1942, the wrath of the Nazis was turned on an unassuming mining village near the steel town of Kladno. On the night of 9 June, Lidice was sealed off, its menfolk shot and its women and children sent to concentration camps, from which few returned. The village was bulldozed and its name erased from the record. After the war, a new Lidice was built a short distance away and the site of the original village became a memorial, with a rose garden of remembrance and a **museum** (open Apr–Oct daily 9am–6pm, Nov–Mar daily 9am–4pm; admission fee) telling the tragic story in bitter detail.

Nelahozeves

On the banks of the Vltava north of Prague, the otherwise ordinary village of **Nelahozeves** has not one, but two attractions, albeit of very different kinds. Music-lovers make their way to the **Památník Antonína Dvořáka** (Dvořák Birthplace Museum; open 1st, 3rd week in month, Wed–Sun 9am–noon, 1–5pm, 2nd, 4th week in month, Wed–Fri 9am–noon, 1–5pm; admission fee), the modest village house where the great composer was born, while rather more visitors head for the **zámek** (open Tues–Sun 9am–noon, 1–5pm; admission fee). After the fall of Communism, this splendid Renaissance castle was given back to its original owners, the princely Lobkowicz family, who completed its restoration and filled it with a magnificent array of objects. Begun in the mid-16th century, the castle is extravagantly sgraffitoed on the outside and has a succession of opulent interiors reflecting the high status of what was one of the kingdom's leading families.

Mělník, Terezín and Litoměřice

Visible from far away across the plain, the castle and parish church of the small historic town of **Mělník** crown the bluff high above the confluence of the Vltava with the Elbe (Labe). With its origins in the 9th century, the castle was the place where the future 'Good King' Wenceslas

(born around 907) was tutored in the ways of Christianity by his grandmother, Princess Ludmila. During the 14th century, Emperor Charles IV revived the local wine industry by importing vines from Burgundy, and, stepping down in terraces from the castle, Mělník's vineyards are still famous, and the wine is on sale in the castle shop. The

Mělník

zámek (open daily 10am–5pm; admission fee) is in a variety of styles ranging from Gothic to Baroque, and has interesting wine cellars. Nearby, the parish church with its landmark tower has a **kostnice** (ossuary).

Within sight of each other, and only separated by the River Labe, the towns of **Terezín** and **Litoměřice** could hardly be more different. For centuries the market centre for the fertile surrounding countryside, historic Litoměřice was one of Bohemia's most important towns, with a vast central square and a wealth of churches. By contrast, Terezín is an ugly upstart, a grim fortress town of barrack blocks, laid out in the late 18th century to protect the northern approaches to Prague. Outside the main walls and moats, the **Malá pevnost** (Small Fortress; open Apr–Oct daily 9am–6pm, Nov–Mar daily 9am–5.30pm; admission fee) served as a political prison in Austro-Hungarian times. The regime was brutal, but nothing like what was to come under the Nazis. In 1941 they expelled all Terezín's inhabitants, and turned the town into what they claimed was a model ghetto. No extermination camp, Terezín nevertheless saw thousands of deaths, and a majority of those incarcerated here were eventually transported to Auschwitz. The **Muzeum Ghetta** (open Apr–Oct daily 9am–6pm, Nov–Mar daily 9am–5.30pm; admission fee) brings home the horror of the place as well as celebrating the unquenchable spirit which made it a centre of creative endeavour, however temporary.

Kutná Hora

On high ground overlooking a winding river valley, this old town was at its peak in the Middle Ages, when it was bigger than London, and the silver extracted from its mines underpinned the prosperity of Prague and the Bohemian royal court. When the silver ran out, the town shrank to less than a third of its former size and became a backwater. There is still plenty of evidence of Kutná Hora's great days, certainly enough to make it one of the most popular day trips from the capital.

The outstanding monument is **Chrám sv. Barbora** (St Barbara's Cathedral; open May–Sept Tues–Sun 9am–6pm, Oct–Apr Tues–Sun 10am–4pm; admission fee). Despite its uncompleted state, this is one of the glories of Central European Gothic architecture. Begun at the end of the 14th century, in the mid-16th century it was given its extraordinary roof in the form of a triple tent by Benedikt Ried, who also designed the beautiful vaulting of the nave. On one side of the street running north from the cathedral is the huge Jesuit College, on the other, above the drop to the river, a line of Baroque sculptures of gesticulating saints. Further along the valley rim, the 15th-century palace known as the Hradek contains a museum of silver, while beyond rises the tower of another major church, **sv. Jakub** (St James). Adjacent to the church is the much-restored power-house of the city's medieval economy, the **Vlašský dvůr** (Italian Court; open Apr–Sept daily 9am–6pm, Mar, Oct daily 10am–5pm, Nov–Feb daily 10am–4pm; admission fee), now housing a museum of minting. It was here that experts brought in from Florence turned out coins like

The cathedral and Jesuit College, Kutná Hora

the Prague *groschen*, legal tender over much of the known world until the 19th century.

In the suburb of Sedlec just northeast of the town, next to a Gothic church made Baroque by the architect Santini, stands one of the country's great curiosities, the **Kostnice** (Ossuary; open Apr–Sept daily 8am–noon, 1–5pm, Nov–Mar daily 9am–noon, 1–4pm), containing a fantastical array of bells, coats of arms and chandeliers, all made from human bones.

Konopiště

The Czech Republic's main motorway connecting Prague to Brno and beyond leads beyond the tatty outer suburbs into attractive countryside rich in parks and castles. At **Průhonice**, almost within sight of the city, the neo-Gothic castle is not open to the public, but is set in one of Central Europe's finest arboretums, with more than 1,000 trees from around the world. Close to the town of Benešov is **Konopiště** (open May–Aug Tues–Sun 9am–5pm, Apr, Oct Tues–Fri 9am–3pm and Sat–Sun 9am–4pm, Sept Tues–Fri 9am–4pm and Sat–Sun 9am–5pm; Nov Sat–Sun 9am–3pm; admission fee). It rivals Karlštejn in its popularity with visitors. Originally a medieval stronghold, it was restored and modernised in the late 19th century by Archduke Franz Ferdinand. Redolent of the last days of the Austro-Hungarian Empire,

Cold-shouldered at the imperial court in Vienna because he had married Sophie Chotek, a mere countess, Franz Ferdinand was happy to hide away in his rural retreat at Konopiště, where he is reckoned to have shot animals by the hundred thousand. He himself perished by the bullet, when he and Sophie were assassinated in Sarajevo in June 1914 by a Serb nationalist, in what is generally considered to be the starting signal for World War I.

Statuary at Konopiště

the interiors seem much as they were lived in by the archduke and his family, while the pervasive decoration with hunting trophies reflects his passion for the chase. A particular highlight is the armoury, one of the finest private collections in the world. Franz Ferdinand re-landscaped the castle park, providing it with a lavish rose garden.

While Konopiště is buried deep in woodland, the castle at **Český Šternberg** (open June–Aug Tues–Sun 9am–6pm, May, Sept Tues–Sun 9am–5pm, Apr, Oct Sat–Sun 9am–5pm; admission fee) sits on a rocky ridge high above the River Sazava, seemingly impregnable against all comers. The castle was begun in the mid-13th century by a member of the Šternberk family, one of the most powerful dynasties in the realm. Under Communism, a Šternberk was allowed to stay on as guide and curator. Today, the restored stronghold is worth a visit for its superb site and its fascinating, often oddly shaped interiors.

A mountain stream in Šumava National Park

SOUTHERN BOHEMIA

From the cool green uplands of the Šumava National Park to the carp-filled lakes of the Třeboň area, southern Bohemia has some of the country's least spoilt and most harmonious landscapes. Astride the trade routes linking Prague to the Germanic lands, the region was very prosperous in medieval times, leaving a legacy of fine building in small towns, none more picturesque than Český Krumlov. Krumlov is over-looked by its great castle, the former residence of the Schwarzenbergs, one of the feudal families who held sway over much of the area until recent times. Their residences stand guard over towns or, like the great mock-Tudor castle of Hluboká, dominate the countryside. In this Bohemian heartland is an array of picture-book villages, often with pretty farmhouses arranged along a street or grouped around a pond. The largest town is České Budějovice, the regional capital and home of world-renowned Budvar beer.

The Way to the South

With a name that resonates throughout Czech history, the medieval hilltop town of **Tábor** guards the main route from Prague to the south. It originated in a religious settlement, based on the encampment set up in 1420 by the fanatical followers of fiery preacher Jan Hus. From here, led by their one-eyed commander Jan Žižka, they sallied forth to spread their beliefs and harry their enemies all over Central Europe. The town still has its bewildering maze of streets and alleyways, laid out thus in order to confuse any invader; it even continues underground in a labyrinth of cellars and tunnels. A small section of these can be explored as part of a visit to the **Husitské muzeum** (Hussite Museum; open daily 8.30am–5pm; admission fee) in Tábor's Old Town Hall, which has displays on the doings of the Hussites and on local history.

An alternative route to southern Bohemia is via **Příbram**, a mining town that grew rich on silver in medieval times, then became notorious under Communism for the uranium worked by forced labour. A covered stairway leads from the town up to the hilltop Marian shrine of **Svatá Hora** (Holy Mountain; open June–Aug daily 9am–5pm, Apr–May, Sept–Oct daily 9am–4pm), one of the country's most important places of pilgrimage. To the east of Příbram, where the River Vltava runs in a deep, wooded valley, two Schwarzenberg castles rise over the surface of the water, much raised since the construction of a dam downstream. First built in the Middle Ages, **Orlík** (open June–Aug Tues–Sun 9am–6pm, Apr, Oct Tues–Sun 9am–4pm, May, Sept Tues–Sun 9am–5pm; admission fee) was remodelled in mock-Gothic style in the 19th century. By contrast, despite its ruinous state, **Zvíkov** (open June–Aug Tues–Sun 9.30am–5pm, May–Sept Tues–Sun 9.30am–noon and 1–4pm, Apr, Oct Sat–Sun 9.30am–noon and 1–3.30pm; admission fee) has retained the uncompromising look of a medieval stronghold, with a guardian tower and gateway.

The castle at Jindřichův Hradec is haunted by a benevolent ghost, the Bilá paní ('White Lady'). Forced to marry against her will, the unfortunate noble-woman Berta of Rožmberk was caught bidding farewell to her sweetheart, and never forgiven by her cruel and jealous husband. Centuries later, she can still be spied wandering the castle corridors, or occasionally dealing out gruel to the town's poor.

Třeboň Region

The countless bodies of water studding the level landscape around the tiny town of **Třeboň** are artificial ponds, mostly dug in the Middle Ages as breeding grounds for carp. Třeboň itself is dwarfed in extent by the great pond on whose banks it stands, the Svět (World) Pond, and the town is the centre of the fishery operations which still dominate the economy of the area. Still guarding the historic centre are walls and gateways, together with the Renaissance **zámek** (open June–Aug Tues–Sun 9am–5.15pm, Apr–May, Sept–Oct Tues–Sun 9am–4pm; admission fee), set in English-style parkland.

Somewhat larger than Třeboň, **Jindřichův Hradec** is also bounded by water. The town is pleasant enough, but the real attraction is the great **zámek** (open May–Sept Tues–Sun 8am–5pm, Apr, Oct Tues–Sun 9am–4pm; admission fee), the third-largest and one of the most fascinating in the country. Starting as a medieval stronghold, it was much rebuilt in Renaissance times, giving it a lovely entrance courtyard with a three-storey loggia and some remarkable interiors. Another high point is the **rondel**, a free-standing rotunda with a steeply pitched conical roof, glorious stucco decoration and perfect acoustics.

Tucked away in deep countryside to the north of Jindřichův Hradec is the castle of **Červená Lhota** (open June–Aug Tues–Sun 9.30am–5.15pm, May–Sept Tues–Sun 9.30am–4pm, Apr, Oct Sat–Sun 9am–4pm; admission fee), one of the country's most popular visitor sights. A ruddy Renaissance cube of a building, it perches on a rock in the middle of a lake, linked to the 'mainland' by a bridge.

České Budějovice

The home of the famous Budvar brewery, the capital of southern Bohemia has numerous other industries, as well as a stately Old Town centred on its arcaded square. On the age-old salt route leading north from Austria, the town was founded in the 13th century by King Ottakar II to remind the often overambitious local lords of the limits of their power. For a while it was Bohemia's third-largest city, and in 1832 became the northern terminus of a pioneering, horse-drawn railway from Austrian Linz, 132km (82 miles) away.

King Ottakar is remembered in the name of the spacious, perfectly rectangular square, **Náměstí Přemysl Otakara II**;

Česke Budějovice, capital of southern Bohemia

Mock-Tudor Hluboká castle

lined with dignified burgher houses, its focal point is the Samson Fountain of 1727. The scale and fine proportions of the square can best be appreciated by climbing the 72m (236ft) **Černá věž** (Black Tower; open 10am–6pm daily July–Aug, Tues–Sun Apr–Jun and Sept–Oct; admission fee), built in 1577 to house the bells of the neighbouring cathedral.

Overlooking the River Vltava just north of Budějovice is one of the country's most popular visitor sights, the huge mock-Tudor castle of **Hluboká** (open June–Aug Tues–Sun 9am–5pm, Sept–Oct Tues–Sun 9am–4pm, Apr–May Tues–Sun 9am–4.30pm; admission fee). Once a royal stronghold erected by Ottakar II, it subsequently became the chief residence of the Schwarzenbergs, who remodelled it in the mid-19th century, shamelessly taking England's Windsor Castle as their model. Beyond the great entrance gateway are 140 elaborately furnished rooms, not all of which are open to the public. The castle's riding school is now the **Alšova jihočeské galerie** (South Bohemian Gallery; open May–Sept daily 9am–noon, 1–6pm, Oct–Apr daily 9–11.30am, 12.30–4pm; admission fee), which houses a rich collection of Gothic masterpieces and an array of 20th-century Czech art.

The pretentiousness of Hluboká's architecture contrasts with the unaffected charm of the traditional buildings of south Bohemia's villages, many of them in 'Peasant Baroque' style. Given UNESCO World Heritage status, the finest collection of them, ranged along the green, can be seen at **Holašovice**, but most villages in the region have good examples.

Český Krumlov and Šumava National Park

Almost entirely enclosed in a loop of the River Vltava, and dominated by a crag-top castle second only to Prague's Hradčany in size, **Český Krumlov** is a tiny medieval jewel that exerts an irresistible charm on its many visitors.

Like Hradčany, Krumlov's **zámek** is virtually a small town in its own right. As well as the 300 or so rooms grouped around its five courtyards, it includes a host of ancillary buildings, including stables, a brewery, pharmacy, salt-house and even a mint, for the castle was the focal point of what was virtually a small kingdom encompassing much of southern and western Bohemia. Its origins lie in a fortress built here in the 13th century, and extended ambitiously by its successive owners. The last of these were the Schwarzenbergs, whose wealth and status were such that they even employed a small private army. Visitors can walk freely through the castle courtyards,

Český Krumlov, wrapped in a loop of the River Vltava

crossing on the way the moat with its captive bears. To get an idea of the extent of the complex and savour a wonderful panorama of the town crouched at its foot, it's worth climbing the **tower** (open Apr–May, Sept–Oct Tues–Sun 9am–4.30pm, June–Aug Tues–Sun 9am–5.30pm; admission fee). Ranging in style from stately Renaissance to comfortable 19th-century, the interiors are so extensive that to see them all you will need to take two tours (open Tues–Sun Apr–May, Sept–Oct 9am–5pm, June–Aug 9am–6pm; admission fee). The **Maškarní sál (Masquerade Hall)** should not be missed, a spacious ball-room from whose walls a host of colourfully attired revellers, painted there in the 18th century, seem about to join in the fun. A further tour is necessary to see the castle's unique Baroque **theatre** (open May–Oct Tues–Sun 10am–4pm; admission fee), still with its original scenery, lighting and wardrobe. Beyond the theatre, the castle grounds include a superb formal garden and a landscaped park with a modern revolving stage.

Within the bend of the river, the town's close-packed streets centre on the main square, with its Plague Column and arcaded Town Hall. Another focal point is **sv. Vít,** the

Shocked by Schiele

Along with Gustav Klimt, Egon Schiele (1890–1918) was one of the luminaries of the Viennese art scene in the early years of the 20th century, producing paintings of extraordinary intensity and unusual frankness in their depiction of the human body. In the summer of 1911, Schiele settled in Krumlov (then known by its German name of Krummau), the native town of his mother. His idyll here came to an abrupt end when the townsfolk threw him out, enraged by his open association with his unmarried girlfriend and by his employment of under-age models. Schiele perished in the terrible Spanish flu epidemic at the end of World War I.

tall-towered Gothic parish church dedicated to St Vitus, while art-lovers are catered for in the **Egon Schiele art centrum** (open daily 10am–6pm; admission fee), named after the Viennese painter, whose mother came from Krumlov.

Along with its counterpart over on the Bavarian side of the mountains, the wonderfully wooded **Šumava National Park** is some-

A nude from the Egon Schiele Art Centre

times referred to as the 'Green Roof of Europe'. Always a thinly settled area, it lost its mostly German population of loggers, herdsmen and glassmakers after World War II, and as a border zone during Communist times was largely off-limits. Today its gently rounded mountains, meadows, lakes and boglands make it a tranquil paradise for walkers and nature lovers.

The valley of the Vltava leads upstream from Český Krumlov, past the castle at **Rožmberk** and the monastery at **Vyšší Brod**, turning sharply northwestwards to **Lipno Lake**. This reservoir is one of the country's most popular recreation areas, the only part of the Šumava to suffer overcrowding. The highest point in the mountains is not far distant; close to the meeting point of the Bohemian, Austrian and Bavarian borders, **Plechy** (1,378m/4,521ft) overlooks the highland lake of Plesné jezero. At the heart of the Šumava is one of Europe's last virgin forests, the **Boubínský prales**; the forest itself is closed to visitors, but it is skirted by a footpath leading to the summit of Boubín (1,362m/3,264ft). Of all the small towns in or around the mountains, the most attractive is **Prachatice**, its historic core still protected by walls and gateways.

WESTERN BOHEMIA

This region of the Czech Republic is rimmed by wooded high-lands making a natural frontier along the border with Bavaria and Saxony, while much of the rest of the area consists of rolling hills and deep forests, thinly inhabited for the most part following the expulsion of the mostly German population after World War II. In a strategic position on the ancient highway between Nuremberg and Prague stands the region's capital, the industrial city of Plzeň (Pilsen), famous as the birthplace of lager beer. Roads lead northwest to the 'West Bohemian Triangle' of spa towns: Karlovy Vary (Carlsbad), Mariánské Lázně (Marienbad) and Františkovy Lázně (Franzensbad). Still basking in the memory of their glory days a century and more ago, the trio remain among the country's great tourist attractions. They are often still referred to by their German names.

Taking the waters in Karlovy Vary

Karlovy Vary (Carlsbad)

Prettily located in a wooded ravine at the confluence of the Ohře and Teplá rivers, **Karlovy Vary** has a dozen main hot springs delivering abundant sulphurous water at temperatures of 42–73°C (108–163°F). The springs were discovered in the 14th century, but it was only later that the spa began to be patronised by Europe's cosmopolitan elite. Its heyday came in the late 19th and early 20th century, when a building boom produced the

> Karlovy Vary's name honours 14th-century Emperor Charles IV, whom legend credits with the town's foundation. A keen huntsman, Charles was enjoying the pleasures of the chase when one of his hounds fell howling into a hot pool. The monarch tasted the water, found it good, received some welcome relief by dangling an afflicted leg into it, and ordered a town be built on the spot.

palatial hotels, ornate villas and extravagant spa facilities that give the town its present opulent character.

At the heart of the spa stand the colonnades from which the healing waters are dispensed. The finest of them is the neoclassical **Mlýnská kolonáda** of 1881, while a modern colonnade houses the **Vřídlo**, a spectacular spring spouting water high into the air at a temperature of 72°C (162°F). Nearby, a Baroque Plague Column, a lovely church by Kilián Ignác Dientzenhofer and the remains of Charles IV's castle give a sense of Karlovy Vary's great antiquity.

A short distance up the River Ohře from Karlovy Vary is the tiny medieval town of **Loket**, almost entirely encircled by a bend in the river, and dominated by its castle. Looking down from its rocky height over the town's curved and sloping main square, the grim medieval **hrad** (open Apr–Oct daily 9am–4.30pm, Nov–Mar daily 9am–3.30pm; admission fee) has historical collections and a good display of local porcelain.

Mariánské Lázně (Marienbad)

While Karlovy Vary's waters are hot, **Mariánské Lázně**'s 40 springs are cool; they emerge from the ground at temperatures between 9° and 12°C (48–54°F) and are used to treat a variety of ailments. And while Karlovy Vary's history goes back to the 14th century, Mariánské Lázně was founded as late as 1808 and generously laid out among spacious parks and gardens. Mariánské Lázně's golden age, like Karlovy Vary's, came in the decades around the turn of the 20th century. Well-heeled guests stayed in the opulent hotels lining one side of Hlavní třída, the boulevard running from the station towards the head of the valley where the main spa facilities are housed.

The town's outstanding monument is the gracefully curving, glass and cast-iron **Kolonáda**, built in 1889, which links the spa gardens to the **Křížový pramen**, the delightful little pavilion of 1811 built over the oldest spring still in use. Germany's all-round genius, Goethe, was an inveterate spa guest, visiting Karlovy Vary on no less than 13 occasions, and it was here in Mariánské Lázně in 1820, when he was already in his seventies, that he wooed the last of his many loves, the 17-year old Ulrike von Levetzov. Goethe is remembered in the **Městské muzeum** (Town Museum; open Tues–Sun 9.30am–5pm; admission fee), which occupies the 'Golden Grape', the house he frequented when here. Among later guests to Mariánské Lázně was Britain's King Edward VII, who caroused with his fellow monarchs between rounds of golf and dalliances with a local girl.

Kolonáda at Mariánské Lázně

The main square in Cheb

Cheb

Only a short distance from the Bavarian border, and centred on its splendid, funnel-shaped main square, Cheb (Eger in German) was the capital of Bohemia's most resolutely Germanic province, the Egerland. This, together with its picturesque townscape of timber-framed and steep-roofed buildings, helps explain its description in old guide books as the 'Bohemian Nuremberg'.

The medieval **castle** (open July–Aug daily 9am–noon and 1–6pm, June, Sept Tues–Sun 9am–noon and 1–6pm, Mar, Oct Tues–Sun 9am–noon and 1–5pm; admission fee) was strengthened by Emperor Frederick Barbarossa in the 12th century, and retains the basic forms of his imperial palace and keep. The main attraction in Cheb, however, is the square. Named after the Czech king George of Poděbrady, it has a brace of fountains and the **Špalíček**, a colourful group of free-standing half-timbered buildings. Nearby, the **Muzeum** (open Apr–Oct

Tues–Sun 9am–12.30pm and 1–5pm, Nov–Mar Wed–Sun 9am–12.30pm and 1–5pm; admission fee) has good historical collections, of which the highlight is the section devoted to General Albrecht von Wallenstein, assassinated here in 1634.

The third of the 'Bohemian Triangle' of spa towns is **Františkovy lázně (Franzensbad)**, established in 1793 in the marshy woodlands just north of Cheb. In its time, Františkovy lázně attracted much the same glittering clientele as its rivals, providing them with elegant lodgings in the houses lining its streets and gentle promenades in the Kurpark and the flat countryside beyond. The focal point of the spa is the **Františkův pramen (Francis Spring)**, the neo-

Plzeň Madonna

classical pavilion covering the spring named (like the town) after Habsburg Emperor Franz II. Nearby is the town's mascot, a chubby bronze cherub holding a fish, the symbol of fecundity; the spa treats gynaecological ailments including infertility.

Plzeň (Pilsen)

Plzeň owes its commercial and industrial renown to its strategic position on the highway between Prague and Bavaria and to the great Škoda engineering works, but for most people it is synonymous with the beer which bears its name. Brewed here since the mid-19th century,

Pilsner Urquell *(see below)* has been often imitated, but never surpassed. The beer's reputation brings many tourists to Plzeň, but the city is well worth a visit in its own right, with the biggest square in Bohemia, the tallest church, plenty of museums and all the vitality of a regional capital.

The city was laid out on a chequerboard plan in the mid-13th century, and stayed relatively small until the 19th, when it became one of the industrial powerhouses of the Austro-Hungarian Empire. In May 1945 it was liberated, like much of western Bohemia, by General Patton's Third US Army, a fact suppressed during Communist times. The main square, **Náměstí Republiky**, is spacious enough to contain the city's tall-towered cathedral. Buildings of various dates and styles line the square, none of them outdoing the gabled Renaissance Town Hall in flamboyance.

The city's most valuable treasure, housed in the Gothic **St Bartholomew's Church**, is the Plzeň Madonna, a delicate marble statue that dates from 1390. Her facial features are incredibly soft, as are the folds in her robe.

Real Pilsner

Plzeň had long been a centre of brewing, when in 1842 the so-called Burgher Brewery was founded by a group of citizens concerned to improve standards. Almost by accident, their Bavarian master-brewer hit on the world-beating formula of a bottom-fermented product, a light, slightly acidic beer, whose character owes something to superlative Bohemian hops, Plzeň's abundant spring water, and the town's network of underground passages, which provide ideal conditions for storage. The reputation of Pilsner beer soon spread, and its formula was widely imitated. To protect the authentic product, it was given the German name of 'Pilsner Urquell', *urquell* meaning 'original' or 'primeval' source ('Plzeňský Prazdroj' in Czech).

On the ring road to the west of the old centre is Plzeň's magnificent **Velká synagóga** (Great Synagogue; open Apr–Oct Sun–Fri 11am–5pm; admission fee), with its twin onion domes second in size in Europe only to Budapest's Great Synagogue. Part of it still used by the city's remaining Jewish community, it now mainly serves as a concert and exhibition hall.

Of Plzeň's several museums, the one predictably attracting most attention is the **Pivovarské muzeum** (Brewing Museum; open Apr–Dec daily 10am–6pm, Jan–Mar daily 10am–5pm; admission fee), which tells visitors everything they could possibly want to know about the city's long relationship with beer. For the real thing, the **Plzeňský Prazdroj** ◀ brewery offers tours of the whole operation and the opportunity to sample the product straight from the barrel (daily guided tour 12.30pm and 2pm; admission fee).

Plzeň's central position makes it a good starting point for many excursions. To the west is one of the country's architecturally most fascinating monastery complexes. **Klášter Kladruby** (Kladruby Abbey; open June–Aug Tues–Sun 9am–5pm, May, Sept Tues–Sun 9am–4pm, Apr, Oct Sat–Sun 9am–4pm; admission fee) dates back to the early 12th century, but it is the 18th-century rebuilding of its church (by Santini) and monastery buildings (by K. I. Dientzenhofer) that command attention. The latter contain fine sculptures by M. B. Braun, while the church demonstrates Santini's masterly synthesis of the Gothic and Baroque styles.

To the southwest, not far from the border with Bavaria, the charming old town of **Domažlice** is the stronghold of the *Chodové*, an independently minded ethnic group who extracted all kinds of privileges in return for guarding the frontier. Their culture, which includes devotion to the art of the bagpipes, can be studied in the town's **castle** (open mid-Apr–mid-Oct Tues–Sun 9am–noon, 1–5pm, mid-Oct–Mar Mon–Fri 10am–noon, 1–3pm; admission fee).

Winter in the Krkonoše (Giant Mountains)

NORTH AND EAST BOHEMIA

An almost unbroken rampart of forested highlands separates northern and eastern Bohemia from neighbouring Saxony in Germany and Silesia in Poland. Shared with Germany, the Krušné hory (Ore Mountains) drop abruptly to the lowlands around the River Ohře, where towns and countryside are slowly recovering from the forced industrialisation of Communist times. On both sides of the gorge cut by the northward-flowing River Labe (Elbe), the sandstone hills have been eroded into fantastical rock formations, some forming the Národní park České Švýcarsko (Bohemian Switzerland National Park). Together with the aptly named and geologically similar Český raj (Bohemian Paradise) further east, they make wonderful walking country. Beyond Liberec, the busy regional capital of northern Bohemia, the uplands attain the status of real mountains; the Krkonoše (Giant Mountains) are the highest in the country, drawing visitors in both summer and winter.

Pravčická brána, Bohemian Switzerland

The Labe Gorge and Bohemian Switzerland

The industrial city and river port of **Ústí nad Labem** has an
enviable location in the winding wooded gorge of the Labe
(Elbe). This stretch of the river, a natural gateway from Saxony to Bohemia, found much favour among the Romantic
artists and writers of the early 19th century; one of their
favourite sights was the crag-top castle of **Střekov**, better
known then by its evocative German name of Schreckenstein.
Even those with little time to spare should take the detour to
the top for the panoramic views of the river in its setting.

Downstream from Ústí, the town of **Děčín** makes a good
base from which to explore the fascinating landscapes of
Bohemian Switzerland. Rising imposingly over town and
river, the **zámek** (open Tues–Sun 9am–noon, 1–5pm; admission fee) has a long history including recent use as a Soviet
army barracks. More than its partly restored interiors, its most
fascinating feature is the Baroque rose garden, artfully cut into

the rock on which the castle is set (open May–Sept Tues–Sun 9am– 8pm, Apr, Oct Tues–Sun 9am–6pm; admission fee). An alternative starting point for excursions is the tourist village of **Hřensko**, on the border with Saxony at the point where the little River Kamenice joins the Labe. Disfigured by countless souvenir stalls, the village has nevertheless kept some of its original charm from the turn of the 20th century. The sandstone bluffs rising over the right bank of the Kamenice form part of the **Národní park České Švýcarsko (Bohemian Switzerland National Park)**. A wooded wilderness of sandstone towers and cliffs and of stream-filled chasms, well provided with both walking and cycling trails, the park is immensely popular, not least with rock climbers. One place where climbing is not allowed is the park's greatest attraction, the **Pravčická brána**, (open Apr–Oct daily 10am–6pm, Nov–Mar Sat–Sun 10am– 4pm; admission fee), Europe's largest natural stone bridge.

Liberec and Around

Glassmaking continues to flourish in northern Bohemia. Two of its main centres are **Kamenický Šenov** and **Nový Bor**, both of which have museums showing the very best of traditional glassware. On a hilltop near Kamenický Šenov, the **Panská skála** consists of an extraordinary conglomeration of basalt columns. A more prominent feature in the landscape is the conical mountain called the **Ještěd**. Rising to 1,012m (3,320ft), its summit is prolonged skywards by a futuristic metal structure housing observation galleries, a restaurant

Liberec Town Hall

> Close to Liberec, the glassmaking town of **Jablonec** is known for its costume jewellery and buttons. The prize exhibit in the town's **Glass and Jewellery Museum** is a 220m (722ft) long necklace put together by local students in a successful attempt to win an entry in the *Guinness Book of Records*.

and cafeteria, and a hotel. The Ještěd overlooks the north Bohemian metropolis of **Liberec**, which under the name of Reichenberg was the largest city in the German-speaking part of Czecho-slovakia. Nicknamed the Bohemian Manchester, the city grew rapidly in the 19th century on the back of its textile industry. It has the buzz of a much bigger city; there's a grand regional museum, the **Severočeské muzeum** (open Tues–Sun 9am–5pm; admission fee) with fine displays of arts and crafts, and an art gallery, the **Oblastní galerie** (open Tues–Sun 9am–6pm; admission fee), whose collections include much good modern Czech painting. The town's most distinctive building is the pompous neo-Renaissance **radnice (Town Hall)**, completed in 1893 at the height of the textile boom to a design remarkably (and deliberately) like that of Vienna's City Hall.

The Krkonoše (Giant Mountains)

Straddling the border between Bohemia and Polish Silesia, these are the Czech Republic's most formidable mountains, a national park since 1963. The highest point is **Sněžka** (1,602m/ 5,255ft), which, like the other summits in the range, is rounded and well above the treeline. The mountain climate is severe, with the country's highest rainfall, low temperatures and frequent fogs, and a walking expedition is not to be taken lightly at any time of the year. A popular hike is to the source of the Labe, one of the rivers which has its origin here. In the last century, acid rain devastated the Krkonoše forests, which then suffered insect attack. The worst of the damage has been removed by felling, and during the long winter season is concealed by a blanket of snow.

Known in German as the Riesengebirge, the Krkonoše gets its Czech (and Polish) name from Krakonoš, a legendary, rather grumpy and capricious giant liable to terrorise travellers in what for long was an almost completely uninhabited region. Tourism began in the late 18th century, when intrepid visitors would stay in a *bouda*, one of the mountain huts which are still a feature of the area. A century later

Hikers in the Krkonoše

came the rise of resorts like **Špindlerův Mlýn**, **Pec pod Sněžkou**, **Janské Lázně** (originally a spa) and **Harrachov** (a glassmaking town). Well equipped with chairlifts and ski-lifts, the mountains now draw the crowds in both the summer and winter months.

The Bohemian Paradise

Closer to Prague than the Krkonoše and equally popular as a walking destination, the **Český raj (Bohemian Paradise)** is a region of extraordinary rock formations set in fragrant pine-woods. As in Bohemian Switzerland, the sandstone here has been eroded into columns, pinnacles and blocky masses divided by deep clefts. Among the most visited areas are the 'rock cities' of **Hrubá skála** and **Prachovské skály**. In places, volcanic intrusions into the sandstone have left prominent bluffs, forming superb sites for castles like **Kost**. Equally spectacular is **Trosky**; its two tall towers built on a brace of basalt rocks form one of the most instantly recognisable silhouettes in the Czech Republic. Another castle, **Hrad Valdštejn**, was the family seat of the great General Wallenstein; it stands just outside the town of **Turnov**, the centre for famous Bohemian garnets. The history of the working of these and other precious stones is dealt with in the town's excellent **Muzeum českého raje** (Museum of the Bohemian Paradise; open May–Sept Tues–Sun 9am–5pm, Oct–Apr Tues–Sun 9am–4pm; admission fee).

Hradec Králové and Pardubice

The historic capital of eastern Bohemia wears two faces. On a rise above the River Labe, **Hradec Králové**'s Old Town comprises one of the country's finest urban ensembles, a funnel-shaped square with church, cathedral, bishop's palace, free-standing bell tower and Town Hall. Below is the early 20th-century New Town, laid out along strictly rational lines by some of the country's leading modern architects. Two institutions are well worth a visit. In the Old Town, the **Galerie moderního umění** (Modern Art Gallery; open Tues–Sun 9am– noon, 1–6pm; admission fee) is a fine example of Czech Art Nouveau architecture, housing an outstanding collection of

the country's modern art. In the New Town, the **Muzeum vychodních Čech** (Museum of Eastern Bohemia; open Tues–Sun 9am– noon, 1–5pm; admission fee) has a fine arts and crafts collection.

Only a short distance down the Labe from Hradec Králové, its great rival **Pardubice** is of similar size and also consists of an Old and New Town. The city is famous for its steeplechase, and notorious for the explosive Semtex. The charming Old Town is laid out around the **zámek** (open Tues–Sun 10am– 6pm; admission fee), the residence of the Pernštejn clan. Its most striking feature is the Knights' Hall, with splendid Renaissance frescoes. The

**Rock city of Hrubá skála
in the Bohemian Paradise**

The flat countryside around Hradec Králové was the scene in 1866 of one of Central Europe's bloodiest and most decisive battles. Often referred to by the town's German name of Königgrätz, and sometimes called the 'first battle of modern warfare', it resulted in the utter rout of the Austrian army by its rival Prussia, whose troops made deadly use of innovative breech-loading artillery.

Pernštejns were also responsible for the **zámek** (open May–Aug Tues–Sun 9am–noon, 1–4pm, Apr, Sept, Oct Sat–Sun 9am–noon, 1–4pm; admission fee) in the town of **Litomyšl**. Fully deserving of its UNESCO World Heritage status, it has an 18th-century theatre in its original state. Composer **Bedřich Smetana** was born in the castle brewery, now a museum (open May–Aug Tues–Sun 9am–noon, 1– 5pm, Apr, Sept, Oct, Sat–Sun 9am–noon, 1–4pm; admission fee).

To the north of Hradec Králové is **Kuks**, a spa created at the turn of the 18th century. For a while a centre of learning, culture and festivity, it was largely destroyed when the Labe flooded in 1740. The imposing remains include a Baroque hospice, an apothecary and a chapel, and above all some superlative statuary of the Vices and Virtues by M. B. Braun. The little hilltop town of **Nové Město nad Metují** is graced with a delightful town square of Renaissance houses, but its great attraction is its **zámek** (open July–Aug daily 9am–5pm, May, June, Sept Tues–Sun 9am–4pm, Apr, Oct Sat–Sun 9am–4pm; admission fee). Originally a Renaissance structure, it was given an astonishing Art Nouveau make-over in the early 1900s. More homogenous in style is nearby **Opočno** (open July–Aug Tues–Sun 9am–11.30am, 12.30–6pm, May, June, Sept Tues–Sun 9am–11.30am, 12.30–5pm, Apr, Oct Sat–Sun 9am–11.30am, 12.30–4pm; admission fee), a magnificent Renaissance castle built around a three-storey arcaded courtyard.

NORTHERN MORAVIA

The two major cities of northern Moravia could hardly be more different. With its fair share of industries, many linked to the rich farmland all around, Olomouc is only outdone by Prague in its number of listed buildings. An ancient town, the seat of rulers and archbishops, it's also a young and lively place thanks to its thriving university. Ostrava is a comparative upstart, founded on the coal mines and steelworks which made it a byword for pollution and degradation. The post-Communist decline of heavy industry may have brought unemployment, but it has improved the environment. The great compensation for living in Ostrava is the presence nearby of the meadows and forests of the Beskydy Mountains, whose vernacular timber architecture and folkways have been carefully preserved in the country's largest open-air museum, at Rožnov pod Radnoštěm. To the north of Olomouc, the Jeseníky Mountains are the highest in Moravia, with forests and little spa towns largely undiscovered by visitors from abroad.

Town Hall tower and astronomical clock, Olomouc

Olomouc

The capital of Moravia until it was sacked by the Swedes in the Thirty Years War, **Olomouc** benefited greatly from

> **Like Prague, the Town Hall of Olomouc has an *orloj*, or astronomical clock. It was damaged in World War II, and after 1945 its original medieval figures were replaced by the present, decidedly proletarian ones in the style of Social Realism.**

the subsequent reconstruction, which gave it the largely Baroque character that so distinguishes it today. The historical centre of the city is laid out around a series of squares. The most ancient of these is Václavské náměstí (Wenceslas Square), with the much-restored cathedral and the 12th-century **Přemyslovský palace** (Přemyslid Palace; open Apr–Sept Tues–Sun 10am–6pm; admission fee). To the west, Náměstí Republiky, like most of Olomouc's squares, is graced by a fine fountain. The heart of the Old Town is further west still, laid out around **Horní náměstí (Upper Square)** and **Dolní náměstí (Lower Square)**. Lower Square has a fountain, but Upper Square has two, one dedicated to Julius Caesar, the city's legendary founder. But what really catches the eye is the 1754 **Trinity Column** – commemorating plague victims – 35m (115ft) high.

Into the Jeseníky

The old town of **Šumperk** serves as a gateway to the Jeseníky Mountains, but a more attractive place to stay is **Velké Losiny**, a spa town with a superb Renaissance **zámek** (open May–Aug Tues–Sun 9am–11am and 1–4pm, Sept Tues–Sun 9am–11am and 1–3pm, Apr, Oct Sat–Sun 9am–11am and 1–3pm; admission fee). Set in parkland, and with a three-storey galleried courtyard, the castle was the base of the powerful Žerotín dynasty. Still turning out wonderful hand-made paper is the nearby 16th-century **Ruční papírna** (Paper Mill; open July–Aug Mon 10am–2pm, Tues–Sun 9am–noon and 12.30–5pm, Apr–June, Sept Tues–Fri 9am–5pm, Sat–Sun 9am–noon and 12.30–5pm, Oct–Mar Tues–Fri 9am–3pm, Sat–Sun 9am–

noon and 12.30–4pm; admission fee). The main road continues north towards the Polish border, climbing up through hairpin bends to the Červenohorské sedlo at 1,010m (3,314ft). To the east is the bleak summit of **Praděd** (1,492m/4,922ft), the highest point in the Jeseníky. Of the little spa towns tucked away in the mountains, the most alluring is **Karlova Studánka**. Guests come here for various treatments, but also to hike, breathe clean air and make the most of the severe winters.

Ostrava

Ostrava, the Czech Republic's third-largest city, is the focal point of a vast industrial conurbation which stretches to the Polish border and be-
yond. The demise of coal and steel has led to severe unemployment as well as to a welcome decrease in the pollution which used to cast a near-permanent pall over the area. The spacious main square, Masarykovo náměstí, still has some of the grand residences of long-dead mine owners, as well as the old City Hall, now the Museum, but Ostrava's finest building is the **Nová radnice** (New City Hall), a splendid Functionalist structure completed in 1930. Anyone with an interest in industrial archaeology should head for the suburb of Petřkovice, where

The Mining Museum at Ostrava

the **Hornické muzeum Pod Landekem** (Mining Museum; open daily 9am–6pm; admission fee) allows visitors to descend deep into a former coal mine.

To the south of Ostrava, **Nový Jičín** is a pleasant enough small town, but its great attraction is its delightful **Kloboučnické muzeum** (Hat Museum; open Apr–Sept Tues–Fri 8am–noon, 1–5pm, Sat–Sun 9am–4pm, Oct–Mar Tues–Fri 8am–noon, 1–4pm, Sun 9am–3pm, Oct also Sat 9am–3pm; admission fee), which is housed in the castle once owned by the Žerotíns. Founded in 1799, the hat factory here produced headgear for the whole of Austria-Hungary, and more than 600 examples are on show. Fewer in number, but just as fascinating, are the road and rail vehicles and aircraft on display in nearby **Kopřivnice** at the town's **Technické muzeum Tatra** (Tatra Museum of Technology; open May–Sept Tues–Sun 9am–5pm, Oct–Mar Tues–Sun 9am–4pm; admission fee).

The Tatra

Named after the highest mountains in Slovakia, Tatra vehicles have been made in Kopřivnice since 1897. In the 1930s, the firm pioneered streamlined cars with rear-mounted, air-cooled engines, a world-beating formula borrowed without permission by the makers of the Volkswagen Beetle. With a cruising speed of 150km/h (93mph), the sleek and silver Tatra 77a was much in demand by Nazi officers and officials during the Occupation, and has since become an icon of 20th-century design. Its post-war successor, the 603, was turned out in substantial numbers until production ended in 1974. Invariably painted black, and of decidedly sinister appearance, it became the limousine of choice of the Communist nomenklatura. Sad to say, it has no successor, and today's notables are chauffeured around in the usual assortment of Audis, Mercedes and BMWs.

The Beskydy

Stretching to the northeast into Poland and Slovakia, the forested Beskydy Mountains rise to their highest point at the summit of Lysá (1,325m/4,347ft), though the most frequented spot is the lower but more accessible **Radhošt'** (1,129m/3,704ft), crowned with a chapel dedicated to the Christian Apostles Cyril and Methodius. The region was settled in the late Middle Ages by Vlachs (Wallachs), wandering herdsmen said to have originated in Romania. The best place to see traditional Wallachian timber architecture is in the town of **Rožnov pod Radhoštěm**, where the excellent

A traditional building at the Wallachian Open-Air Museum

Valašské muzeum v přírodě (Wallachian Open-Air Museum) is to be found. The most extensive of its kind in the country, it has three sections: the **Dřevěné městečko** (Little Wooden Town; open May–Sept daily 9am–5pm, Jan–Mar, Oct Tues–Sun 9am–4pm, Apr Tues–Sun 9am–5pm; admission fee), with timber buildings brought here from local towns and villages; the **Valašská dědina** (Wallachian Village; open mid-May–Aug daily 9am–5pm; Sept daily 10am–5pm; admission fee), a reconstruction of a typical mountain village; and the **Mlýská dolina** (Mill Valley; open May–Aug daily 9am–5pm, Sept daily 10am–5pm; admission fee), where the power of water to perform useful tasks is demonstrated in a series of mills.

SOUTHERN MORAVIA

Centred on the Czech Republic's vibrant second city, Brno, southern Moravia looks southward towards Austria and the Danube. Fertile soils and a warmer climate than the rest of the country favour fruit-growing and the production of wine, the latter centred around the border towns of Znojmo and Mikulov. Folk traditions have persisted longer here, particularly in Slovácko, the area bordering on Slovakia. A constellation of towns offers urban pleasures in abundance, from the Renaissance jewels of Telč and Slavonice in the southwest to the glorious gardens of the episcopal town of Kroměříž. As in the rest of the country, castles and great houses abound, among them the crag-top stronghold of Pernštejn. Separating Moravia from Bohemia, the uplands of the Českomoravská vysočina remain relatively unknown,

A typical vineyard at Salov, near Znojmo

but offer broad horizons, deep woods, and peace and quiet, as well as a number of architectural treats like Santini's pilgrimage chapel at Žďár nad Sázavou.

Brno

Succeeding Olomouc as the capital of Moravia after the Thirty Years War, Brno is an ancient place, built on two hills, on one of which stands the cathedral, on the other the infamous Špilberk prison. By the 19th century the city's busy textile industry caused it to be dubbed the 'Austrian Manchester',

> Brno's Old City Hall is home to two curiosities. The Brno Dragon – in fact, a stuffed crocodile – was presented by Archduke Matthias in 1608. To win a wager, the Brno Wheel was built from scratch and rolled here from Lednice, 40km (25 miles) away, all in a single day.

while in the 20th its innovative buildings made it a beacon of modern architecture. There's plenty to see in Brno's traffic-free centre, where buildings of all periods sit comfortably together and you can enjoy all the atmosphere of a genuine provincial capital.

The city centre's bustling main axis is Masarykova, which leads from the imposing railway station to **Náměstí Svobody (Liberty Square)**, lined with a mixture of buildings old and (relatively) new, among them the Dům u čtyř mamlasů (Four Oafs Building). Another focal point of city life is **Zelný trh (Cabbage Market)**, its stalls grouped around the pulsating stonework of the Baroque Parnassus Fountain. Filling one corner of the square is the **Moravské zemské muzeum** (Moravian Museum; open Tues–Sat 9am–5pm; admission fee), among whose displays is the famous, flagrantly female figurine known as the Venus of Věstonice, some 27,000 years old. Less healthy-looking are the rather more recent figures on view in the nearby **Kapucínská hrobka** (Capuchin Crypt),

Brno's Gothic cathedral

where a quirk of ventilation has kept the mummified corpses of monks and their benefactors in a near-perfect state of preservation.

Rising over this part of town are the slender twin spires of the **cathedral**, built in Gothic style, Baroquised after being damaged in the Thirty Years War, then re-Gothicised in the 19th century. Beyond the cathedral there's a fine view from the landscaped ramparts.

Back towards the centre of town, the **Stará radnice (Old City Hall)** has a number of fascinating features, notably the striking Gothic portal with a drooping central pinnacle. Inside the entrance there are two objects of curiosity value: the Brno Dragon and the Brno Wheel *(see page 75)*.

The climb up Brno's second, higher hill leads past the **Uměleckoprůmyslové muzeum/UPM** (Decorative Arts Museum; open Wed–Sun 10am–6pm, Thur 10am–7pm; admission fee), rivalling its namesake in Prague for superlative displays of the applied arts. The neighbouring **Pražákův palác** (same opening hours) shows works from its rich and extensive collection of 20th-century Czech art. At the summit squats the **Špilberk** fortress, for long the main prison for the political enemies of Austria-Hungary. You can shudder at the horrors of the **Kasematy** (Dungeons; open May–Sept Tues–Sun 9am–6pm, Oct–Apr Tues–Sun 9am–5pm; admission fee) and revive your spirits in the **Muzeum města Brna** (Brno City Museum; open May–Sept Tues–Sun 9am–6pm, Apr,

Oct Tues–Sun 9am–5pm; Nov–Mar, Wed–Sun 10am–5pm; admission fee), which has extensive displays on city history from the 11th century onwards. Beyond the city centre, the **Vila Tugendhat** (open Wed–Sun 10am–6pm; admission fee; book in advance, tel: 545 212 118) of 1930 is a cool and elegant Modernist dwelling of glass, steel and concrete, a masterpiece by the German architect Mies van der Rohe.

Moravský Kras (Moravian Karst)

The classic day excursion from Brno is to the Moravian Karst, the wooded limestone massif to the north of the city, with an array of caves, sink-holes and underground rivers. The most visited cave is the **Punkevní jeskyně**, with spectacular stalactites and stalagmites, the extraordinary 138m (453ft) deep Macocha Abyss, and a section of underground river which can be explored by boat.

Punkevní jeskyně cave

Pernštejn and Žďár nad Sázavou

Its walls and towers rising sheer from the forests, **Hrad Pernštejn** (open July–Aug Tues–Sun 9am–5pm; May–June, Sept 9am–4pm, Apr, Oct Sat–Sun 9am–noon, 1–3pm; admission fee) is the archetypal medieval stronghold. Dating originally from the 13th century, it was altered over the centuries, its harsh exterior eventually concealing comfortable 19th-century living quarters. Crowning another hilltop, called Zelená hora (Green Mountain), just outside the nondescript town of Žďár nad Sázavou, is one of the country's most unusual buildings. The **Hřbitovní kaple sv. Jana Nepomuckého** (St John of Nepomuk Pilgrimage Chapel; open May–Oct Tues–Sun 9am–5pm; admission fee) is the work of the architect Santini, built in 1722 as part of the Church's growing cult of Nepomuk.

Austerlitz

East of Brno is the small town of **Slavkov**, better known by its German name of Austerlitz. On 2 December 1805, it was in the countryside around the town that one of the decisive battles of the Napoleonic Wars was fought, when the French army routed a larger Austro-Russian force. The story of the battle is told at the **Mohyla míru** (Peace Mound; open July–Aug daily 9am– 6pm, May, June, Sept daily 9am–5pm, Apr Tues–Sun 9am– 5pm, Oct–Mar Tues–Sun 9am–3.30pm; admission fee). Napoleon oversaw the signing of the armistice in Slavkov's **zámek** (open May–Sept Tues–Sun 9am–5pm; Apr, Oct–Nov Tues–Sun 9am–4pm; admission fee).

Kroměříž

Kroměříž is dominated by its big Baroque palace, the summer retreat of the archbishops of Olomouc. The **Arcibiskupský zámek** (Archbishops' Palace; open May–Sept Tues–Sun 9am–5pm, Apr, Oct Sat–Sun 9am–4pm; admission fee) has magnificent interiors, including a great hall in white and

Kroměříž gardens, Květná zahrada

gold. The archbishops amassed a fine picture collection, some of which, with works by Van Dyck, Cranach and Titian, is still here. On the outskirts of the town, the splendid **Květná zahrada** (Flower Garden; open daily, summer 7am–7pm, winter 7am–4pm) remains in all its original Baroque glory, with radiating avenues centred on a circular pavilion and an immense Roman colonnade.

Luhačovice and Slovácko

Nestling in the wooded foothills of the White Carpathian Mountains close to the Slovak border is the spa of **Luhačovice**, essentially a 20th-century creation, when the architect Dušan Jurkovič designed many new buildings in his characteristic style, a synthesis of Art Nouveau and folk motifs. South of Luhačovice, the Slovácko area owes its name to its mixed ethnic character. It's a region where the local dialect is as much Slovak as Moravian, and folk traditions are very much alive.

Vranov nad Dyjí near Znojmo

Mikulov and Znojmo

One of the main centres of Moravian wine production is **Mikulov**, perched on a limestone outcrop adjacent to the Austrian border. Appropriately enough, the **zámek** (open May–Sept Tues–Sun 9am–5pm; Apr and Oct Tues–Sun 9am–4pm; admission fee) houses in its cellars what locals claim is Europe's biggest wine barrel, with a capacity of over 100,000 litres (66,000 gal). In the rolling countryside to the east of the town stretch the vast estates of the **Lednicko-Valtický areál**, for six centuries the jewel in the crown of the powerful Liechtenstein family. Around their castles at **Lednice** and **Valtice** is a park-like landscape of immense aesthetic and ecological value, strewn with an extraordinary array of ornamental buildings.

Like Mikulov, **Znojmo** is a historic hilltop frontier town, with very much the same wine traditions. Its tight-knit medieval pattern can best be appreciated from the tall tower of its Town Hall, while beneath the streets is a labyrinth of catacombs. The town's great treasure, to be found in the castle grounds, is the **Rotunda** (open June–Sept Tues–Sun 10am–5pm, May Sat–Sun 10am–5pm; admission fee), which contains the country's finest and best-preserved Romanesque frescoes. Znojmo makes a good base for exploring the deep and winding valley of the River Dyje, a popular holiday area for Czechs. Apart from countryside activities, the main attraction here is the Baroque **zámek** of **Vranov nad Dyjí** (open July–Aug Tues–Sun 9am–6pm, May–June, Sept Tues–

Sun 9am–5pm, Apr– Oct Sat–Sun 9am–4pm; admission fee), perched on an impossibly high crag above the river.

Telč and Slavonice

Of all the smaller historic towns in the Czech Republic, **Telč** is considered by many to be the most exquisite. It consists essentially of two gateways, a castle, and its glory, the square lined with perfectly preserved Renaissance and Baroque town houses, nearly all with fanciful gables or pediments. The **zámek** (open May–Sept Tues–Sun 9am–noon, 1–5pm, Apr, Oct Tues–Sun 9am–noon, 1–4pm; admission fee) has many delights, the most fascinating of which is the gorgeous funerary chapel of the lord of the castle, Zachariáš z Hradce.

To the south of Telč, on the Austrian border, **Slavonice** is an irresistible little place, with a wonderful variety of exuberantly sgraffitoed buildings in its streets and squares.

Telč

WHAT TO DO

OUTDOOR PURSUITS

Ever since the late 19th century when they founded an organisation – the *Klub českých turistů* – to promote their interests, the Czechs have been among the world's keenest hikers. Over the years, the KCT has covered the country with a dense network of waymarked trails, making walking one of the best ways of getting to know the many delights of the Czech landscape. Virtually every object of interest has a trail leading to it, usually starting from some convenient point like a bus or railway station or town square. National parks and other protected areas are particularly well provided with paths, including a number of long-distance trails such as the ridgewalk in the Krkonoše Mountains or the 120km (75-mile) route through the Šumava National Park from Lipno Lake to the town of Klatovy. Accommodation along such routes is plentiful, but so are your fellow-walkers, at least in summer, and it is advisable to book your room in advance. In mountain country like the Krkonoše, where weather can be extreme and quite unpredictable, all the usual rules should be observed: wear appropriate weatherproof clothing and robust footwear; take maps, compass and whistle; and be willing to retreat to base if conditions appear threatening. Insects can be troublesome in summer, and walkers should arm themselves with repellent. As in other parts of East-Central Europe, encephalitis-causing ticks can be a problem in wooded areas, and should be protected against by specific repellent and by covering up appropriately.

Paths are identified by waymarks in colour (blue, green, red or yellow, edged above and below in white), with fingerposts at crossing points. They are also clearly shown on the excellent 1:50,000 scale maps covering the whole of the country.

Walking is of course the best way of exploring towns, especially where there has been extensive pedestrianisation, as is the case in Prague. Here, there is little point in taking a coach tour, as the historic centre is relatively compact, and there are numerous offers of accompanied walking tours, often run by individuals with expert knowledge and a good line in anecdotes.

Cycling

Exploring the country by bike has increased enormously in popularity in recent years. Most minor rural roads are not heavily trafficked and are suitable for cycling, and the network of dedicated cycle tracks is increasing every year. There are now well over 17,000km (10,600 miles) of numbered *cyklotrasy*, identified by coloured signs (blue, green, red or white, edged above and below in yellow, and showing the number of the route). The first long-distance cycle route connected Prague with Vienna, and other trails follow the River Elbe (Labe) between the capital and Dresden or run along the banks of the Morava. The tranquil, flat, pond-studded countryside of southern Bohemia and southern Moravia is particularly suited to a cycling holiday, while new, themed trails have been devised

Rock Climbing and Caving

Northern Bohemia abounds in sandstone cliffs and columns of varying difficulty, notably in the Český raj (Bohemian Paradise) and České Švýcarsko (Bohemian Switzerland). Nearer Prague is the Český kras (Bohemian Karst) area of limestone rocks. Note that these are all protected landscapes, and climbers should inform themselves locally about restrictions on their activity. The Bohemian Karst offers a number of underground attractions, but the most spectacular caverns are those of the Moravský kras (Moravian Karst) to the north of Brno.

threading through the vineyards of southeastern Moravia or linking places of interest to beer-drinkers in the Beskydy uplands. Bicycles can be hired in many places and can be carried on trains for a modest fee. Repair shops are fairly common. The most useful map for cyclists, with all routes clearly marked, is the one at 1:100,000 scale.

Boating on Lipno Lake

Water Recreation

Lakes and reservoirs attract the kinds of activities – bathing, sailing, windsurfing, rowing – that the sea provides for in other countries. The largest such water body is the artificial Lipno Lake in southern Bohemia, and other extensive lakes along the Vltava include those formed by dams at Orlík and Slapy. The River Dyje in southern Moravia has been dammed in a similar way and is equally popular, while Máchovo jezero (Mácha Lake) in northern Bohemia even has a sandy beach. Such areas are well provided with facilities of all kinds, including the hire of equipment. Note that motor boats are banned. Perhaps of greater interest to visitors from abroad is the chance of canoeing along the more scenic stretches of some of the country's rivers. The upper reaches of the Vltava are particularly attractive, both above and below Lipno Lake, and its tributaries the Berounka and Sázava are also well worth exploring. In northern Bohemia, the River Ohře has mildly challenging stretches near Kynšperk nad Ohří. Upstream from Olomouc, the River Morava flows through a tranquil, bird-rich protected landscape of woods and water meadows, while above and below

Winter sports in the Krkonoše

Uherské Hradiště in south-eastern Moravia the same river, including a canalised section, has been adapted for water-based recreation, with ample facilities for boat hire.

Czechs are keen anglers, and there are plenty of opportunities in lakes and rivers to fish for such species as trout and carp. Enquire locally about permits.

Winter Sports

The mountains and uplands running almost all the way along the borders of the Czech Republic provide suitable conditions for winter sports, which enjoy great popularity. The season lasts from December to March, though snow cannot be guaranteed at any time. There are more than 40 resorts distributed around the various ranges, from the Šumava in the southwest right around to the Jeseníky and Beskidy in northern Moravia. Most have facilities for downhill and cross-country skiing, snowboarding and sledging. A few places are able to supplement natural snowfall with snow-making machines. Informal cross-country skiing is enjoyed all over the country, a favourite area being the Česko-moravská vysočina (Czech-Moravian uplands).

In terms of downhill skiing, nothing quite comes up to the challenging runs of the Swiss Alps, but the Krkonoše resorts like Špindlerův Mlýn and Pec pod Sněžkou have slopes which will satisfy the expectations of experienced skiers. When conditions are good, the more popular resorts can become overcrowded, with long queues for lifts and pressure on accommodation.

Golf and Tennis

Frowned on in Communist days as a sport for plutocrats, golf has made great strides since 1989 and enjoys considerable prestige. The oldest course in the country is the one patronised in the early years of the 20th century by King Edward VII in the course of his visits to Carlsbad. Among the more recently laid out 18-hole courses, the best are probably those at Mariánské Lázně and Karlštejn, while the most extensive is at Mladé Buky in the Krkonoše Mountains.

By contrast, tennis was actively promoted under the old regime, producing stars like Lendl and Navrátilová. After football and ice hockey, it remains the country's favourite sport, and there are tennis courts in most towns and cities.

Spa Visits

Recovering your health in the agreeable surroundings of a spa has a long tradition in the Czech lands, not least because of the profusion of mineral springs. The golden age of the spa was in the late 19th and early 20th century, when considerations of health took second place to the social and cultural delights provided in abundance in such world-renowned places as Karlovy Vary (Carlsbad) and Mariánské Lázně (Marienbad). Under Communism, spas took on a more egalitarian tinge, with grand hotels supplemented by hostels for the more deserving members of the proletariat. Since 1989 there has been a revival and expansion of activity in the country's 40 or more spa centres. The emphasis is now as much on relaxation, fitness and 'wellness' as on the cure of medical conditions, though nearly all the spas offer specialised treatments for particular problems. Staying in a spa, or at least spending part of your holiday in one, is certain to be a pleasant and stimulating experience; most have excellent leisure and recreational facilities, full cultural programmes, and are often set in lovely landscapes within easy reach of many other attractions.

Bohemian glass

SHOPPING

Even during the Communist era, the Czech lands continued to offer their visitors a range of fascinating traditional products, all of which continue to be produced and which still make excellent souvenirs. Otherwise the country is well on the way to matching Western countries in the range and quality of merchandise available; Prague in particular has become something of a shopper's paradise, with retail outlets ranging from flagship stores with their standardised products to intimate individual boutiques with unique offerings. While the former readily accept credit cards, the latter may not; check before committing yourself to a purchase. Virtually everything you may want to buy is available in the capital. However, in the case of traditional products, it may be more interesting as well as cheaper to visit the places where they are made, such as a north Bohemian glassware centre like Harrachov or Kamenický Šenov, where it may also be possible to view the process of manufacture.

Things to Buy

Glassware and porcelain. Bohemia has been a centre of glass production for centuries, and lead crystal decanters, vases, bowls and glasses are of fine quality and offer excellent value. The famous firm of Moser presents a superb array of items in its palatial Prague showrooms. Porcelain of equal refinement is also available, particularly that made by the famous Karlovy Vary factory.

Garnets. Seductive, deep-red Bohemian garnets have been extracted in the area around Turnov in northern Bohemia for many years. Gracing rings, necklaces and bracelets, they can be found in several outlets in Prague or in Turnov itself.

Toys and puppets. Puppet theatres have given rise to a lively marionette-manufacturing sector, though most of the appealing puppets on show in shops have been made as souvenirs. A marionette intended for real performances is in a different league altogether, and will not be cheap. Drawing on similar skills and traditions, wooden toys are also of superior quality.

Recordings. Czech musicality is reflected in the number and quality of recordings available in various forms. CDs of the music of Czech greats such as Dvořák and Smetana are of high quality and offer excellent value. Other music worth sampling includes folk music and *dechovky*, the rousing marches and polkas played by the country's innumerable brass bands. Film buffs may be thrilled to find past masterpieces of the Czech cinema like *A Blonde in Love* or *Closely Observed Trains*, now reissued on DVD with English subtitles.

Puppets for sale

Books. Books are published in abundance, and most large bookshops now have foreign-language sections with good translations of Czech classics and excellent illustrated books of the cof-

Antiques shops in Prague

fee-table kind. In Prague, there seems to be an *antik-variát*, a second-hand book-shop, around every corner, and most towns have at least one of these fascinating institutions, which sell not only old books in various languages but an amazing array of ephemera such as maps, old tourist brochures, badges and postcards.

Antiques. The counterpart to the antiquarian bookshop is the *starožitnosti*, the antiques shop, the offerings of which can range from the un-saleable to the overpriced, though there are usually a fair number of bargains in between, particularly from the Art Deco and Communist periods. Rare or expensive items may require an export permit.

Food and drink. As well as being a centre of porcelain manufacture, Karlovy Vary turns out the ultra-thin wafers known as *oplatky* along with the oddly shaped, spouted porce-lain vessels sipped from by spa guests taking the cure. Also from Karlovy Vary is *Becherovka*, a bitter-sweet liqueur made from an age-old secret recipe. From the orchard country of Moravia comes *slivovice*, plum brandy, perfectly acceptable in its commercial form but out of this world if you are fortu-nate enough to get access to a privately distilled supply. Czech beer is the best in the world and still extraordinarily cheap, though obviously difficult to transport. Moravian wines, particularly whites, are steadily improving in quality, and the Czech equivalent of champagne is quite acceptable and far cheaper than the original. Bohemian vineyards are few and far between, the main centre of production being at Mělník.

Food specialities worth taking home are few in number. Famous Prague ham is sold in tins, and you may find a particular kind of sausage takes your fancy.

Contemporary art and design. Contemporary artworks – paintings, graphic works and sculpture – can be viewed and purchased from numerous galleries. As well as a particular kind of Czech whimsy which does not appeal to all tastes, there is much else besides, sometimes of great originality and high quality. Artistic glassware in particular is well worth investigating.

Purpose-made souvenirs. Over-the-top souvenirs can be found all along the tourist trail. Lining roadsides close to the border are regiments of plastic garden gnomes of the most garish kind, sold by Vietnamese stallholders to a seemingly insatiable tide of German shoppers. In Prague, there has been an outbreak of establishments offering 'Slavonic' souvenirs such as Russian dolls and enamelled boxes which have only the most tenuous connection with anything Czech.

ENTERTAINMENT

Musical life thrives in the Czech Republic, not only in Prague but in provincial centres as well, and lovers of classical music, opera and ballet are unlikely to escape temptation. Popular culture and entertainment is vibrant, too, with a lively 'scene' in many towns, though none can match the capital where every possible taste is catered for in a wide array of venues. Details of events are readily available from tourist information centres, and for Prague there are useful listings in the monthly English-language 'Prague Events', as well as in the far more comprehensive *Přehled kulturních pořadů v Praze* in Czech.

Music, Opera, Theatre

Classical music, opera and ballet can be enjoyed in the larger towns, in the case of Brno and Olomouc in 19th-century theatres of great lavishness. Prague has several superb auditoriums, including no fewer than three that stage performances of opera: the **National Theatre** is the most opulent, though the **State Opera** comes a close second, and the historic late 18th-century **Estates Theatre** is where Mozart conducted the premiere of his *Don Giovanni*. The National Theatre is also the home of the national ballet and theatre companies, and its modern extension, the *Nová scéna*, is one of the main venues of **Black Light Theatre**, that uniquely Czech fusion of mime, pantomime, dance, music and virtuoso lighting effects. The **Rudolfinum** is the home of the Czech Philharmonic Orchestra, while the Prague Symphony Orchestra is based in the **Municipal House**, whose Smetana Hall sees the annual rendering of the master's *Má vlast* which launches the Prague Spring Festival. Visitors from abroad will find themselves tempted by the numerous performances of popular classics in historic settings such as the Mirror Chapel of the Klementinum or amid the Baroque splendour of St Nicholas' Church. In summer, there are outdoor concerts in the delightful ambience of Mozart's Bertramka and the Renaissance garden of the Wallenstein Palace. Many of the provincial music festivals which are such a feature of the country's cultural life make use of equally appealing settings.

Rock, Pop, Jazz

Rock and roll, pop music and jazz can be heard all over the country, though the greatest concentration of talent is in the capital. Keep an eye open for posters and flyers, as well as checking out the offerings of established venues in Prague such as Reduta (for jazz) and Palác Akropolis (alternative music). The delights of dance music can be found virtually everywhere, though the virtuoso DJs mostly confine themselves to the bigger towns and, of course, Prague.

Folk Music and Brass Bands

Folk culture is alive and well in parts of the country, though its role in everyday life is much diminished. The most folksy region is undoubtedly southern Moravia, where traditions are assiduously cultivated and the cimbalom is the typical instrument. In Bohemia, folkways are most prominent in the western region of Chodsko, with its miniature capital **Domažlice**, where the bagpipe reigns supreme.

The stirring sound of a brass band is a taste that Czechs share with their German neighbours, and marches and polkas were favoured by the Communist regime as a counter-blast to the subversive sounds of rock and roll. Open-air performances by military and other bands are frequent.

Moravian folk dancers in Borsice

Sign on a Prague puppet theatre

CHILDREN

Travelling with children in the Czech Republic is little different from elsewhere in Europe. The larger hotels will usually be able to provide babysitting and other facilities. Rules of conduct have traditionally been rather more strict than in countries further west, and uncontrolled or exuberant behaviour in public places such as restaurants may meet with disapproval. Young people are expected to give up their seats on public transport to their elders and to the infirm.

With its many castles, its weird rock formations and its fairy-tale capital, the country is sufficiently 'different' to grab children's interest for much of the time. Many sights are associated with stimulating stories and blood-curdling legends, often recounted in children's books. Properly told, the tale of the Golem should keep young imaginations busy for a while.

Getting around in unusual ways can be an experience in its own right. Many children will be unfamiliar with the trams which ply the streets of many of the big towns, notably Prague. Stand at the back for the best view. A horse-drawn carriage ride can also be fun, as can a trip on a branch railway line. A walk in the mountains can be enhanced by a ride in a chairlift. In Prague, the funicular to the top of Petřín Hill is a good prelude to the child-friendly attractions at the top, among them a planetarium, mirror-maze and mini Eiffel Tower. Prague has a zoo, and there are others at Brno and Jihlava. Black Light Theatre will appeal to some, and puppetry is always a hit, particularly the performances put on by the National Marionette Theatre.

Calendar of Events

1 January New Year celebrations.

February *Masopust:* pre-Lenten carnival.

April–May *Flora Olomouc:* international garden festival, held in the capital of Czech horticulture.

Easter Monday Young men chastise girls with braided willow whips and receive painted Easter eggs as a reward.

May *Ride of the Kings:* traditional procession followed by three-day folk festival in Vlènov in southeastern Moravia; *Prague International Marathon:* the race follows what must be one of the most picturesque marathon routes in the world.

May–June *Prague Spring:* this music festival is one of the most important events in the international classical music calendar, lasting for three weeks and featuring musicians of the highest calibre.

June *Strážnice Folk Festival:* performers from all over the world have attended this major folk music event in Strážnice, southern Moravia, ever since its inauguration in the 1940s.

June–July *Smetana's Litomyšl International Opera Festival:* held over two weekends in the composer's home town.

July *Carlsbad International Film Festival:* a high point in the international cinematic calendar.

Mid-July *Colours of Ostrava:* world music festival.

August *Strakonice International Bagpipe Festival.*

Mid-Sept–early Oct *Pilsnerfest Beer Festival:* beer-lovers converge on Plzeň (Pilsen), the home of Pilsner; *Prague Autumn:* international classical and popular music festival.

October *Prague International Jazz Festival:* a week of first-rate jazz performances; *Velká pardubická:* the Pardubice steeplechase is the country's most prestigious racing event.

5 December *Eve of St Nicholas:* accompanied by a devil and an angel, St Nicholas chides naughty children and rewards the good.

December *Christmas markets:* all sorts of seasonal gifts and food are sold, including live carp for Christmas dinner.

EATING OUT

Traditional Czech food is based on a limited range of ingredients and is intended to sustain body and soul rather than form the basis of a sophisticated eating experience. Ignoring contemporary dictates of healthy living, it revels in heavy meals of meat, nourishing soups, potatoes, and above all dumplings, which feature as much in desserts as in main dishes. In the past, the best food of this kind was prepared at home according to grandmother's own recipes, with restaurant offerings running a very poor second. Nowadays good traditional cooking, or an updated interpretation of it, is widely available, as is international cuisine of every possible kind, at least in Prague.

Pastries are plentiful, and belie their calorie content with their tempting lightness. Czech beer ranks among the world's best and accompanies most meals, though local wines are improving and are now frequently served in restaurants.

WHEN AND WHAT TO EAT

Breakfast (*snídaně*) is a frugal meal when eaten at home, consisting of coffee, a slice or two of tasty rye bread with cheese or ham, and maybe a piece of strudel, preferably home-made. Tea is usually drunk without milk, and many people favour a herbal variety. Turkish coffee, where hot water is simply poured onto coffee grounds, is rarely drunk nowadays. Hotel breakfasts are more sumptuous, almost always presented in the form of a self-service buffet.

Lunch (*oběd*) is eaten earlier than in many countries and may well be the main meal of the day, unless plans have been made to dine out in the evening. The usual starter is soup (*polévka*), which comes in bewildering varieties, among them simple broths or substantial potato soups. Tripe

Diners with a view, Letná Park

soup is recommended as a useful pick-me-up for those still suffering the after-effects of the previous evening's excesses. The main course will invariably incorporate a good helping of meat, of which the runaway favourite is pork *(vepřové maso)*, though it is run a close second by beef, often in the form of *svíčková na smetaně*, fillet or sirloin topped with a slice of lemon, a spoonful of cranberries, and swimming in an abundant cream sauce. The pig enjoys a special status in Czech cooking, and even when reared in mass, its meat is likely to be tastier than anything you are used to. A high point of the year is the *zabíjačka*, when the whole family takes part in the slaughter of a lovingly nurtured porker and the subsequent conversion of every last morsel of the animal into something delicious to eat. In the restaurant you will most likely be served with pork roasted *(pečené)* or presented as a schnitzel *(řízek)*. Whatever meat you have ordered, it will almost always be accompanied by a generous dollop of sauce or gravy, destined to be soaked up by potatoes, or more likely, by the ubiquitous dumplings *(knedliky)*. Dumplings can be made from flour, bread, potatoes or semolina, with added yeast, baking powder, eggs, milk or sugar. Every self-respecting cook has their own way of preparing these essential accompaniments to good eating, and inevitably, the best and lightest are made at home. They come in the shape of an elongated loaf, which is cut into slices by a wire, never by a knife.

There are plenty of alternatives to pork and beef, among them veal *(telecí maso)*, chicken *(kuře)*, duck *(kachna)* and goose *(husa)*, the last-named usually kept for special occasions. Game, too, is plentiful, including venison *(srnčí maso)*, pheasant *(bažant)* and partridge *(koroptev)*. Ocean fish is eaten less than in coastal countries, but there are plenty of trout *(pstruh)* and carp *(kapr)*. Carp are raised in the

Roast pork, bread dumplings and red and white cabbage

ponds of the south of the country, netted in their millions in December, and sold from tanks and barrels in the streets. Kept in the bath at home, they are killed at the last moment before being cut into steaks, breaded and fried as the centrepiece of Christmas Eve supper. If you choose carp from the menu, you will need to beware its many bones.

Vegetables are not one of Czech cooking's stronger points, though greenery in the form of broccoli has

Living life without meat remains a puzzle to most Czechs, and vegetarians still tend to be offered fried cheese (*smážený sýr*) and chips (*hranolky*) over and over again. However, the presence of many expatriates, at least in Prague, has led to an improvement in the situation, and as well as 100 percent vegetarian establishments, there are now many restaurants that offer a range of meat-free dining options.

made a modest appearance on menus. The great staple is cabbage (*zelí*), plain or red or in the form of sauerkraut, its reputation boosted by recent research revealing its range of near-miraculous nutritional properties.

The range of desserts is relatively limited, and most lunchers content themselves with soup and a main course. The favourite is undoubtedly pancakes (*palačinky*), filled with cottage cheese, fruit or nuts and often served with a chocolate sauce. Fruit-filled dumplings are a substantial alternative, and there is always ice cream.

Dinner (*večeře*), if taken at home, may well be something much more modest than lunch. Because Czechs start their working day early, they tend to go to bed early and eat early in the evening, not ideal conditions for enjoying large and lavish meals at the end of the day. So supper might consist simply of a sausage, some ham or cheese, bulked out with bread, accompanied by a gherkin or two and followed by some sort of dessert. A restaurant dinner is likely to follow the pattern of lunch, though perhaps with a cold starter rather than soup and with the emphasis on a more adventurous main course than run-of-the-mill pork-dumplings-cabbage (*vepro-knedlo-zelo*).

Snacks Alternatives to the ever-increasing number of Western-style fast-food outlets include the sausages on sale from street stands, along with the altogether healthier option of delicious little open sandwiches (*obloženeé chlebičky*) obtainable at delicatessens. These consist of a single slice of bread covered with a mixture of ingredients, perhaps including slivers of ham, salami, hard-boiled egg and fish roe, plus potato salad, a slice of tomato or gherkin, and a squirt of mayonnaise. Sausages come in a number of forms. The favourite is probably the Frankfurter-like *párek*, often sold in pairs (as *párky*). A *vuřt* is bigger and tastier, while a *klobása* is bigger still, coarse-textured and extremely greasy. Sausages are usually served with a splash of mild mustard and a slice of bread.

WHERE TO EAT

Food of reasonable quality can be found all over the country, though opportunities for fine dining tend to be limited to the larger towns and above all to Prague, where every conceivable kind of cuisine is now to be found.

A *restaurace*, a conventional restaurant, will vary widely in terms of price, ambience and type of food. At the lower end of the scale are straightforward establishments making most of their money serving lunches to office workers, usually with a set menu offering excellent value. At the upper end are palatial premises with menus of great sophistication and prices to match. Some of the best restaurants of this kind are those attached to the more prestigious kind of hotel, in Prague and elsewhere.

Elegant surroundings in the Café Imperial

A *vinárna* is literally a wine restaurant, but may differ little from the more refined kind of *restaurace,* except possibly in the length and pretentiousness of its wine list. Special care may have been taken to provide an atmospheric ambience.

A *hospoda* is a pub, where the main activity of beer-drinking does not exclude unpretentious meals, often at a bargain price. Be aware that Czechs accompany their consumption of beer with that of tobacco, and the thick atmosphere in most *hospody* has to be accepted as part of the experience. Some of the best traditional Czech cuisine can be found in the updated pubs of the Kolkovna group (owned by Plzeňský Prazdroj breweries).

A *kavárna* is a café. As elsewhere in Central Europe, café culture here reached a peak of sophistication in the early years of the 20th century, when cafés were the haunt of writers, intellectuals and their hangers-on. Something of this atmosphere can still be found in Prague, where a number of famous cafés maintain their traditions. Coffee and cakes are the staples, though light meals may be served as well. The new generation of cafés which has sprung up is more North American in inspiration.

WHAT TO DRINK

Excellent beer *(pivo)* is brewed throughout the country, with seasoned drinkers swearing by their local product rather than the better-known Prazdroj (Urquell) from Plzeň or Budvar from České Budějovice. Most beers are of the Pilsner type, somehow combining lightness with a full flavour, though dark beers are brewed as well, notably on the premises of Prague's famous old pub, U Fleků. Draught beer is to be preferred to the bottled variety. It is invariably served in half-litre glasses. When visiting a pub, a certain etiquette should be observed. It is quite acceptable, after checking that a seat is free, to sit down at a table already occupied by other drinkers. You need

Why Burčák Does You Good

At some point during September, signs appear in the windows of pubs and bars announcing the arrival of *burčák*. This is the term used to describe the cloudy, half-fermented liquid whose character lies somewhere between grape juice and wine. Said to be high in vitamin B complex and rich in essential minerals and sugars, *burčák* packs quite a kick, despite only having half the alcohol content of mature wine (around 5 percent compared with 11–12 percent). One reason for *burčák*'s sometimes surprising effect is that fermentation continues inside the body. Devotees claim all kinds of benefits from its consumption, while pointing out that to enjoy them you should aim at downing an equivalent volume to the blood in your system. The name *burčák* is protected under EU law, and can only be made with Czech and Moravian grapes from defined regions.

not order a drink; the waiter will set one down in front of you without being asked, and will supply refills until stopped. Wish your companions *Na zdraví!* (To health!) as you raise your glass. The waiter (rarely waitress) will note down how many glasses you have drunk, and you pay on leaving, making up the total to a round figure rather than leaving a substantial tip.

A glass of Budvar

Czech wine *(víno)* is something of a national secret, and very little is exported. There are vineyards in Bohemia, notably around the little town of Mělník, but the majority of Czech wine is in fact Moravian, from the vineyards that extend between Brno and the Austrian and Slovak borders. White *(bílé)* wine is produced in greater quantity than red *(červené)*. Quality is variable but has improved in leaps and bounds over recent years. Sparkling wines include Bohemia Sekt.

Also from Moravia come fruit brandies, foremost among them the variety made from plums *(slivovice)*, generally reckoned to cure most ailments if taken in moderation. Originating from Bohemia, specifically from Karlovy Vary (Carlsbad), *Becherovka* is a herbal liqueur originally intended to be part of the spa cure; it is usually served as an aperitif, as is the sweet but strong *Stará myslivecká*, the equivalent of German *Jägermeister*.

In a country with many natural springs, it is not surprising to find varied kinds of mineral water *(minerální voda* or *minerálka)*; one of the best is Mattoni from Karlovy Vary.

To Help You Order…

Please, may I see the menu?	**Prosím, mohu vidět jídelní listek?**
I am a vegetarian.	**Jsem vegeterián/vegeteriánka.** (m/f)
The bill, please.	**Zaplatím, prosím.**
I would like…	**Prosím…**

beer	**pivo**	meat	**maso**
bread	**chléba**	milk	**mléko**
butter	**máslo**	mineral water	**mineralku**
cheese	**sýr**	salad	**salát**
coffee	**kávu**	sugar	**cukr**
dessert	**moučník**	tea	**caj**
egg	**vejce**	wine	**vino**
ice cream	**zmrzlinu**		

…and Read the Menu

bažant	pheasant	**klobása**	sausage
brambory	potatoes	**knedlíky**	dumplings
buchty	sweet dumplings	**králík**	rabbit
		kuře	chicken
drůbež	poultry	**květák**	cauliflower
fazole	beans	**kyselé zelí**	sauerkraut
guláš	goulash	**okurka**	gherkin
houby	mushrooms	**prstruh**	trout
hovězí	beef	**rajské jablka**	tomatoes
hrušky	pears	**rýže**	rice
husa	goose	**špenát**	spinach
jablka	apples	**srnčí**	venison
jahody	strawberries	**štika**	pike
játra	liver	**šunka**	ham
jehněčí	lamb	**švestky**	plums
kachna	duck	**telecí**	veal
kapr	carp	**vepřové**	pork

HANDY TRAVEL TIPS

An A–Z Summary of Practical Information

A

ACCOMMODATION (see also CAMPING, YOUTH HOSTELS and the list of RECOMMENDED HOTELS on page 127)

There is no shortage of places to stay in the Czech Republic, and standards have improved beyond recognition since the end of Communism. The range extends from luxurious palaces offering every conceivable kind of comfort, to basic pensions, campsites and hostels, with reliable two- and three-star hotels in between. Prague is particularly well provided with establishments at the upper end of the scale, less so with budget options. Even the most forbidding-looking Communist-era block is likely to have been modernised, and it is becoming rare to find a hotel where the rooms are not provided with en-suite facilities. Older establishments have almost all been completely refurbished, and there are plenty of opportunities to stay in historic buildings of the Art Nouveau and other periods. The one- to five-star rating system in use is self-regulating, but usually gives a good idea of the kind of accommodation on offer. The capital generally is considerably more expensive than elsewhere in the country, where rates are well below the European average. Finding a room is rarely a problem, though Prague is busy at all times of the year, and booking in advance is advisable.

Hotel prices usually refer to the cost of a room per night and may be expressed in euros. Breakfast, invariably arranged as a buffet, is normally included in the room rate, but this is not always the case and should be checked. A local tax may be added to the bill. Most establishments accept credit cards for payment. Note that telephone calls made from the room are almost always charged at several times the normal rate. Access for disabled visitors is good in new buildings, very variable otherwise.

Camping is very popular, with hundreds of sites all over the country *(see page 109)*. Another inexpensive option is to stay in a private room (look for signs offering *ubytování*, or, in German, *privat* or *Zimmer*). There are mountain huts in the Krkonoše range. For longer stays, apartments can be rented.

Do you have a single/ double room, please?	**Prosím, mate jednolůžkový/ dvoulůžkový pokoj?**
With bath/shower	**s koupelnou/se sprchou**
What is the rate per day?	**Kolik stojí za den?**
Is breakfast included in the price?	**Je snídaně v ceně?**

AIRPORTS

The main airport is Prague-Ruzyně, with direct flights to and from most major European cities as well as a few intercontinental destinations. Airports at Ostrava, Brno and Karlovy Vary have a limited number of international flights. The only internal flights are those linking Prague with Ostrava and Brno.

Ruzyně is 20km (12 miles) from the centre of Prague. Taxis are a convenient but relatively expensive way to get to the centre, and are operated through a kiosk in the arrivals hall. Some hotels will arrange for guests to be met by private taxi, but this will be more expensive still. Many international travellers use the minibus service run by the CEDAZ company; the minibuses go from the airport to Dejvická Metro station (from where it is only a few stops to the centre), to a stand in Náměstí Republiky in the city centre, or for an extra fee to any central hotel. The least expensive option is to take a city bus to Dejvická or Zličín Metro stations; tickets can be bought in the arrivals hall.

Where do I get the bus/taxi to the city centre/airport?	**Odkud jede autobus/taxi do centra/na letiště?**
How much is the fare to the centre?	**Kolik stojí do centra?**

B

BUDGETING FOR YOUR TRIP

A trip to the Czech Republic can cost as much or as little as you wish. Local wages and salaries are a fraction of Western European rates, and many prices are calculated with this in mind. It is therefore possible for visitors to the country to live very cheaply, provided they stay in modest hotels, eat in restaurants frequented by local people and get around by public transport. By contrast, spending nights in luxury hotels, dining in upmarket restaurants and hiring a car or taking conducted tours can cost as much as or more than anywhere else.

Accommodation. The cost of a double room in a mid-range hotel outside Prague is likely to vary between Kč900 and Kč1,800. Expect to pay twice or three times as much in the capital.

Public Transport. Train travel is inexpensive, averaging out at less than Kč2 per kilometre, and bringing first-class travel (fares about 50 percent higher) within the scope of a modest budget. Long-distance coach fares are comparable or somewhat lower. Urban buses and trams and the Prague Metro are also very good value; a single ticket allowing multiple transfers in Prague costs Kč20.

Taxis. The official rate in Prague is Kč28 per km with a basic fee of Kč40. Rates outside Prague are marginally less.

Car Hire. The rates charged by the main international rental companies are at the same level as elsewhere (at least Kč1,800 per day, Kč7,000 per week). Local firms may charge considerably less.

Eating Out. A two-course midday meal at an unpretentious but good restaurant can cost under Kč100, a sumptuous dinner at a top Prague establishment 20 times as much or more. A half-litre of beer in a pub can be had for as little as Kč22, while the (smaller) bottled product of the same brewery served in a restaurant could be as much as Kč90.

Entertainment. Theatre and concert tickets are inexpensive, especially if purchased at the box office rather than through an agency.

Sightseeing. Entry to museums and galleries is inexpensive, particularly for students and the elderly with appropriate identification.

C

CAMPING

Some campsites are very basic, others well provided with facilities. All represent good value. As well as offering a place to pitch a tent or park a camper van, many have chalets and 'bungalows'. Most sites are open between May and September.

CAR HIRE (RENTAL)

Most of the main international car-hire companies operate in the Czech Republic, with desks at Prague airport. They are supplemented by numerous local firms. It is usually cheaper to book a car in advance of your trip. Hotel desks will arrange car hire, though they are unlikely to use the cheapest firms. Check carefully what is included in the basic rental and what additional insurance cover will cost. Drivers must normally be over 21 years old and have held a full licence for more than a year.

I'd like to hire a large/ small car	**Chtěl bych si vypúčit velké/ malé auto**
For one day/a week	**na jeden den/týden**
Please include full insurance	**Prosím, započítejte plné pojištění**

CLIMATE

In the middle of the European continent, the Czech Republic's weather is determined by both continental and oceanic influences. From Russia come cold winds and snow, while weather systems originating in the Atlantic bring mild air and frequent rainfall. Summers are warm, though invariably interrupted by thunderstorms. Winters are cooler than in Western Europe, and are almost always accompanied by snowfall, especially on the higher ground of the country's mountainous rim. Spring and autumn are marked by changeable conditions. The countryside is at its best and freshest in late spring and early summer, while Prague is welcoming at almost any time of the year.

		J	F	M	A	M	J	J	A	S	O	N	D
Max.	°F	50	52	64	73	82	88	91	90	84	71	57	50
	°C	10	11	18	23	28	31	33	32	29	22	14	10
Min.	°F	9	10	18	28	36	45	48	46	39	28	23	14
	°C	-13	-12	-8	-2	2	7	9	8	4	-2	-5	-10

CLOTHING

If arriving in summer, visitors should add something rainproof to their wardrobe and bring along a warm layer for cool evenings. A jacket or coat is advisable for spring and autumn. Winter cold means that really warm outdoor wear is essential, plus gloves and a warm hat. Stout shoes will reduce wear and tear on feet unused to the cobblestones likely to be encountered in city sightseeing, and weatherproof clothing and footwear are needed for walks in the mountains. Be prepared to leave your shoes at the door if invited into someone's home.

Czech men and women tend to dress informally, and smart casual wear is quite suitable for attendance at the theatre or opera or if dining in a fine restaurant.

CRIME AND SAFETY

The Czech Republic is a relatively safe country, and you only need take the usual precautions, though be aware that petty theft and car crime are common. Leave valuables in the hotel safe, and don't tempt thieves by leaving items of interest on show in your car, which should be parked in a secure car park where possible, especially overnight. Pickpockets are active in areas popular with tourists, so carry valuables in inside pockets and keep bags close to your body. Identity documents are covetable items, and scams involving a false policeman (in plain clothes) asking to see your passport have been reported. If challenged in this way for no good reason, demand to be taken to a police station.

Despite their impressive consumption of beer, Czechs rarely indulge in riotous drunken behaviour in public, and this type of problem is generally confined to those parts of Prague frequented by young visitors from abroad.

Report thefts and incidents to the police, if only to obtain the necessary evidence to make an insurance claim. It makes sense to have a photocopy of your passport and a record of the numbers of your credit and other cards.

CUSTOMS AND ENTRY REQUIREMENTS

The 2004 entry of the Czech Republic into the European Union has meant the reduction of red tape to a minimum. EU citizens need only an identity card (or passport in the case of the UK) valid for 180 days beyond the date of entry to the country (90 days for citizens of Australia, Canada, the US and New Zealand). Information about visa requirements for nationals of other countries can be obtained from embassies of the Czech Republic or by visiting <www.mfa.cz>.

There are no restrictions on the import or export of foreign currency, nor on items for personal use. The export of valuable art objects or antiques requires a permit.

D

DRIVING

To drive your own car in the Czech Republic you will need a valid driving licence, a vehicle insurance certificate, a national identity sticker, a red breakdown triangle, spare light bulbs and a first-aid kit. The headlights on a car with right-hand drive must be adapted with a beam converter kit. Non-EU citizens will need a vehicle registration document. To drive on motorways and similar roads you must purchase and display a sticker (or *vignette*), valid for various periods (15 days for Kč200). Stickers are obtainable at all entry points to the country and at filling stations.

Driving Conditions. The road system is well developed, and road conditions are generally good all over the country. Main roads are well engineered and maintained, though often heavily trafficked, and the motorway network is steadily being extended. Signposting is good, though less so on minor roads. Road signs are of the standard European type. Drivers from Britain should take particular note of the priority sign, a yellow diamond on a white background. This indicates that you are on a road with priority over traffic joining from the right. The same sign with a black line through it indicates the end of the section with priority. Warning of roadworks ahead may be somewhat cursory. Driving in towns can be complicated by the presence of trams and by extensive stretches paved in granite setts or cobblestones, which are slippery when wet. Be aware that the accident rate is well above the European average.

Rules and Regulations. Drive on the right and overtake on the left. The rigorously enforced speed limits are 130km/h (80mph) on motorways, 90km/h (56mph) on ordinary main roads, and 50km/h (31mph) in built-up areas (indicated by the place-name sign). Seatbelts must be worn, and children under 12 may not sit in the front seat. Headlights must be lit (dipped) at all times. Give way to trams and to pedestrians on crossings and when turning right. Drivers with the slightest trace of alcohol in their bloodstream face heavy penalties.

Fuel. Fuel is somewhat cheaper than in most European countries. Filling stations are plentiful, and many incorporate small supermarkets. Credit cards are generally accepted.

Parking. Finding a place to park can be difficult in larger towns, particularly in Prague, where a car is more of a hindrance than a help in any case. Always ensure you have parked legally and paid any necessary parking charge, as police and parking attendants are vigilant. The park-and-ride facilities close to Metro stations on the outskirts of Prague are a useful alternative to braving the labyrinth of city streets.

Jednosměrný provoz	One-way traffic
Na silnice se pracuje	Roadworks
Nebezpeči	Danger
Nevstupujte	No entry
Objížďka	Diversion
Opatrně/pozor	Danger
Pěší/zóna	Pedestrian zone
Snížit rychlost/zpomalit	Slow down
Úsek častých nehod	Accident black spot
Vchod	Entrance
Vychod	Exit
Full tank, please	**Plnou nádrž, prosím**
Super/unleaded/diesel	**super/bezolovnatý/nafta**
I've broken down	**Mám poruchu**
There's been an accident	**Stala se nehoda**
May I park here?	**Mohu zde parkovat?**

Assistance. In case of problems on the road, dial 1240 for help from Autoklub Bohemia Assistance. All accidents must be reported to the police: call 158.

E

ELECTRICITY

The standard is 220V, 50-cycle AC. Plugs are the standard Continental two-pin round type, and British and North American appliances need an adaptor.

EMBASSIES AND CONSULATES

Australia: Solitaire Building, Klimentská 10, Prague 1; tel: 296 578 530.
Canada: Muchova 6, Prague 6; tel: 272 101 800.
Ireland: Tržiště 13, Prague 1; tel: 257 530 061.
New Zealand: Dykova 19, Prague 3; tel: 222 514 672.
UK: Thunovská 14, Prague 1; tel: 257 402 111.
US: Tržiště 15, Prague 1; tel: 257 530 663.

Where is the British Embassy?	**Kde je britské velvyslanectví?**

EMERGENCIES

If you are close to your hotel it may make sense to seek help from the hotel reception.

Police	158
Fire	150
Paramedics	155

Fire!	Hoří!
Help!	Pomoc!
Stop thief!	Chyt'te zloděje!

G

GAY AND LESBIAN TRAVELLERS

While homosexuality is legal in the Czech Republic, attitudes in many places remain conservative if not actively homophobic. The centre of gay life is Prague, where there is a lively scene, details of which are contained in the bimonthly magazine *Amigo*.

GETTING THERE

By Air. A flight is usually the most convenient and often the least expensive way of getting to the Czech Republic unless your starting point is in a neighbouring country. Most flights serve the country's main airport, Prague-Ruzyně, though there are some international flights to and from other airports *(see also AIRPORTS, page 107)*.

The national carrier is Czech Airlines (*České aerolinie – ČSA*), which has direct flights to and from many European cities and a limited number of intercontinental destinations, including New York-Newark. It works in partnership with other airlines to serve other North American destinations including Montreal and Toronto. Other important intercontinental destinations are linked to Prague via a single change at a European hub such as Frankfurt. Most major European carriers operate flights from their capital cities to Prague.

The following airlines fly to Prague from British airports: bmibaby, British Airways, ČSA, EasyJet, flyglobespan, Jet2 and Thomsonfly. Ryanair flies from London-Stansted to Brno.

By Rail. The national rail company, České Drahy (ČD), operates international services in cooperation with the railways of neighbouring countries. There are direct links to cities in Austria, Germany and several Eastern European countries, and a single change of train brings other destinations within reach. Travel from Britain via the Channel Tunnel normally involves at least two changes, and is only worth considering for those wanting to visit other destinations en route.

By Road *(See also DRIVING, page 112)*. The Czech Republic is linked to all its neighbours by good main roads, and to Germany by the D5 (Prague–Nuremberg) and D8 (Prague–Dresden) motorways. Prague is about 1,150km (713 miles) from the car-ferry port of Calais with its frequent sailings from Dover. A thrice-weekly overnight car ferry links Harwich to Cuxhaven, about 1,000km (620 miles) from Prague.

Prague and other Czech cities are connected to numerous destinations in Europe, including London, by long-distance coach services, many of them operated by Eurolines, <www.eurolines.com>.

GUIDES AND TOURS

The standard of services for tourists from abroad tends to be in proportion to the number of visitors attracted to any one place. Thus in remote areas there may be little more than a tourist information centre keeping uncertain hours, while Prague is almost over-provided with tours of every possible kind, from trips around the city in a vintage automobile to an excursion in an air-conditioned luxury coach to a nearby castle. Some of the best value is offered by individual walking tours.

H

HEALTH AND MEDICAL CARE

The Czech Republic has a generally good reputation for medical care, and if you are unfortunate enough to fall ill you should be reasonably well cared for. Emergency medical treatment is free of charge for EU citizens, though you may have to pay for medicines. British subjects should provide themselves with a European Health Insurance Card (forms available from post offices, online at <www.ehic.org.uk> or tel: 0845 606 2030) before travelling. Citizens of non-EU countries should ensure that they are covered by a private insurance policy. Such insurance is worth considering in any case, to cover any longer-term problems and to ensure repatriation if necessary.

Minor health problems can often be solved by visiting a pharmacy (*lékárna*), identified by a green cross.

An ambulance can be called by dialling 155.

HITCHHIKING

Hitching a lift and giving one is widely practised in the Czech Republic. Hitchhikers congregate on main roads leading out of town, showing their hoped-for destination by displaying its vehicle registration letters on a piece of cardboard (CB for České Budějovice, KV for Karlovy Vary, etc.). The usual risks and precautions apply. Note that the ladies standing by the roadside in certain areas bordering Germany are unlikely to be bona fide hitchhikers.

HOLIDAYS

Government offices, banks, post offices and many businesses close on the following national holidays:

1 January	*Nový rok*	New Year's Day
March/April	*Velikonoce*	Easter Monday only
1 May	*Svátek práce*	May Day (Labour Day)
8 May	*Den osvobození*	Liberation Day (VE Day)
5 July	*Den slovanských*	Day of the Slav Apostles
	věrozvěstů Cyrila	Cyril and St Methodius/
	a Metoděje	Introduction of Christianity
6 July	*Den Jana Husa*	Day of Jan Hus
28 September	*Den české státnosti*	Day of Czech Statehood
28 October	*Den vnzniku*	Foundation Day of First
	Československa	Czechoslovak Republic
17 November	*Den boje za svobodu*	Freedom and Democracy Day
	a demokracii	
24 December	*Štědrý večer*	Christmas Eve
25 December	*Vánoce*	Christmas Day
26 December	*Den sv.Štěpana*	St Stephen's Day

L

LANGUAGE

Visitors familiar with any of the Slavonic languages will find written Czech fairly straightforward to understand, though the spoken language is another matter. Many of the people you are likely to come into contact with will speak at least some English or German, but, as in any foreign country, it is always appreciated if the visitor has tried to master a few basic words and phrases. The Czech alphabet has 33 letters, with for example *c* and *č* counting as different sounds. In the Czech language, the stress is always given to the first syllable. Here are tips on the pronunciation of a number of sounds:

c	as ts in tsetse
č	as ch in church
ch	as ch in Scottish loch
ě	as ye in yes
j	as y in yellow
ň	as n in Canute
ř	as rs in Persian
š	as sh in shine
ž	as s in pleasure

Do you speak English/ German?	**Mluvíte anglicky/ německy?**
I don't speak Czech	**Nemluvím česky**
Good day/evening/night	**Dobrý den/Dobrý večer/ Dobrou noc**
Please/Thank you	**Prosím/Děkuji**
Sorry	**Promiňte**
Goodbye	**Na shledanou**

M

MAPS

Excellent maps for walking and cycling are published for the whole country at 1:50,000 scale and for many areas at 1:25,000 scale. An invaluable driving companion is the *Autoatlas Česká Republika* 1:100,000 scale, published by Freytag & Berndt, which shows every road in the country and includes several city plans. The Marco Polo plan of Prague at 1:6,000 scale shows the historic centre in wonderfully clear detail, while the 1:12,000 plan by the same publisher includes much of the capital's suburban area. The 1:23,000 plan published by Prague City Transport shows every Metro station and bus and tram stop in the built-up area. Tourist information centres in towns and cities usually provide some sort of free plan.

MEDIA

Most hotel rooms are equipped with a TV set capable of receiving a range of international channels, often including CNN, Sky and BBC News 24. Czech TV2 has early-morning news in English, and there is English-language news on the radio on 92.6FM. The BBC World Service can be heard on 101.1FM.

Foreign newspapers can be bought from kiosks in major cities, usually the day after publication, but they may be difficult to find elsewhere. The weekly *Prague Post*, founded immediately after the Velvet Revolution of 1989, is an invaluable source of listings as well as news and comment.

MONEY

The currency of the Czech Republic is the crown or *koruna* (Kč), which is divided into 100 virtually useless hellers *(halíř)*. Notes come in denominations of 5,000, 2,000, 1,000, 500, 200, 100 and 50Kč, and there are coins of 50, 20, 10, 5, 2 and 1Kč and 50 hellers.

Currency Exchange. Banks and savings banks are widely distributed and most have an exchange desk (*směnárna*). They offer a better rate of exchange/commission than the kiosks to be found along the tourist trail, particularly in Prague. Bank opening hours vary, but are usually from 8am to 4pm Monday to Friday, with possibly a lunch break in smaller towns. Street kiosks stay open as long as there is any chance of business.

Credit and Debit Cards. Credit cards are not yet as widely accepted in the Czech Republic as in Western Europe, but they can normally be used to pay hotel bills, for meals in classy restaurants and for major purchases. Automatic teller machines (ATMs) are widely distributed, but before leaving check with your bank that your bank card is valid for use in the Czech Republic. The charges for such transactions vary considerably between banks, and should also be checked.

Traveller's Cheques. These offer a safe way of carrying cash and can be exchanged at banks, but stick to the major issuers. Note that traveller's cheques will not be accepted as payment in shops, restaurants and hotels.

O

OPENING HOURS

Shop opening hours are very variable. Some smaller establishments keep to the times established under Communism, opening as early as 7am in the morning and closing at 5pm or 6pm and noon on Saturday. More general hours are between 8am/9am and 6pm Monday to Friday, and until early Saturday afternoon. Department stores, hypermarkets and shops in malls keep far more liberal hours and may even open on Sunday; the same applies to souvenir shops and other establishments serving tourists.

P

POLICE

The police most likely to be encountered by travellers are: National Police, in blue-and-grey uniforms and green-and-white patrol cars; Municipal Police, usually in black; and Traffic Police, with white caps. Police officers do not enjoy particularly high esteem among their compatriots, but are generally helpful to foreigners. The emergency telephone numbers are 156 for Municipal Police and 158 for National Police.

> Where is the police station?   **Kde je policejní stanice?**

POST OFFICES

The offices of the national postal service, Česká Pošta, are widely distributed, but only the main post offices offer the whole range of services. If it is only stamps that you need, your hotel can probably provide them, and they can also be bought at tobacconists and news-stands. Letter boxes are orange or orange and blue in colour. Post offices are open from Monday to Friday 8am–5pm, and on Saturday 8am–noon.

> Where is the nearest post office? **Kde je nejbližská pošta?**

PUBLIC TRANSPORT

Air. The only internal flights link Prague with Brno and Ostrava and are geared to the needs of business travellers.

Rail. The national rail operator is České Drahy (ČD; Czech Railways), which runs almost all the country's train services. The rail network is comprehensive, linking not only the main cities and towns but many smaller places as well. Types of train vary widely, ranging from fast expresses (SuperCity/SC, EuroCity/EC and InterCity/IC) – which have the latest type of comfortable rolling stock – to extremely slow local trains *(osobní vlak)*, consisting of a single, noisy and bumpy railbus. After a few teething problems, a fleet of high-speed Pendolino tilting trains has considerably reduced journey times between Prague and Olomouc/Ostrava and Brno/Vienna/Bratislava. Fares are inexpensive and reliability is generally good. Larger railway stations may have a few English-speaking staff. Arrival *(příjezd)* and departure *(odjezd)* are displayed on overhead information boards and on posters (white for arrivals, yellow for departures). Clear information not just on rail travel, but on all forms of public transport, is also available on the internet at <www.cd.cz> or <www.jizdnirad.cz>.

Coach Services. Long-distance coaches serve most places of any importance, and are often faster as well as cheaper than trains. Timetables are complicated, and many services are scheduled for the convenience of working people and weekenders rather than foreign tourists. Information is available from bus station offices (where they exist), and from timetables pasted up at stops. Tickets should be purchased where such offices exist, otherwise from the driver. Tourist information centres can be a useful source of timetable details. Standards of comfort vary from basic to luxurious, and reliability is generally good.

Urban Transport. Local buses serve every village and hamlet as well as towns. Larger towns have trolleybuses and trams as well as buses, providing a comprehensive transport network. Only Prague has a (mostly underground) Metro. Urban public transport systems are usually fully integrated, with tickets permitting transfer from one mode to another within defined zones and periods of time. Larger cities usually have some sort of night service. Tickets can be obtained from kiosks, machines, some hotels, and sometimes, not always, from the driver, when they may be more expensive (as fares are low by international standards, this is hardly likely to make much of a dent in your holiday budget). Taxis are numerous and not expensive, as long as they adhere to official rates. This is not always the case in Prague, where overcharging is common, and visitors are recommended not to use taxis parked at stands but to call reliable radio taxi companies such as AAA Taxi, tel: 140 14.

Where is the railway/ bus station?	**Kde je železniční/ autobusové nádraží?**
I want a (tram/rail) ticket to…	**Prosím, jízdenku/lístek do…**
Standard/first class	**Druhá/první třída**
Return ticket	**Zpáteční jízdenka**
Does this train/tram/ bus stop at…?	**Staví ten vlak/tramvaj/ autobus v…?**

R

RELIGION

Thanks to the sucess of the Counter-Reformation, by far the most important Church in the Czech Republic is the Roman Catholic Church, followed at some remove by Protestant groups such as the Church of Evangelic Brethren and the Hussite Church. The Orthodox Church also has a number of followers. The minuscule post-Holocaust Jewish population has been supplemented by a small number of immigrants, and there is a tiny Muslim presence. However, the majority of Czechs, possibly as many as 60 percent, consider themselves agnostic or unbelieving. English- and German-speaking visitors will find churches offering services in their languages in Prague.

T

TELEPHONES

The national telephone system was completely overhauled a few years ago by Český Telecom and is generally reliable. Phone numbers consist of nine digits, which should all be used even when you are dialling within the same area code. For directory enquiries dial 1180, for international enquiries 1181. To call abroad, dial the international access code 00, followed by the country code, the area code (without the initial 0 for UK numbers) and the subscriber's number. The country code for the Czech Republic is 420.

The most convenient way to telephone while in the Czech Republic may well be by using your own mobile phone, but check with your provider about the cost of calls. If your stay is a long one, consider renting a phone locally.

Most public phones now take telephone cards, obtainable in various denominations at news-stands, tobacconists, post offices and petrol stations. Telephoning from your hotel may be convenient, but will be expensive.

TIME ZONES

The Czech Republic is on Central European Time (CET), which is one hour ahead of GMT. The clocks go forward one hour at the end of March and back again at the end of October.

TIPPING

At restaurants, a service charge may be added to the bill, in which case you need not leave a tip, though if you are paying in cash it is customary to round up the total. Otherwise 10 percent is a reasonable amount. Rounding up also applies to trips by taxi. Lavatory attendants expect a crown or two, and hotel porters should be given Kč15–20 per item of luggage carried.

TOILETS

Public toilets are few and far between and may not always be in sparkling condition. A fee may be payable. The best idea is to plan your sightseeing with this in mind and schedule café and restaurant stops accordingly.

Muži/Páni	Men/Gentlemen
Ženy/Dámy	Women/Ladies

TOURIST INFORMATION

For information before travelling, contact Czech Tourism at the following addresses, or visit <www.czechtourism.com>:

Canada 410 Bay Street, Suite 1510, Toronto, Ontario M5H 2Y4; tel: 416 363 99 28, fax: (01) 416 363 02 39.
United Kingdom 13 Harley Street, London W1G 9QG; tel: 020 7631 0427, fax: 020 7631 0419.
United States 1109-11 Madison Avenue, New York NY 10028; tel: 212 288 0830, fax: 212 288 0971.

Czech Tourism's headquarters in Prague is at: Vinohradská 46 (PO Box 32), 120 41 Prague; tel: 221 580 111, fax: 224 247 516.

Local tourist information centres are distributed around the country and are generally very helpful, though the printed information available is variable in quality. In Prague, Pražská informační služba (PIS) has a number of centres and provides an excellent service including finding accommodation and booking tickets. Among tour operators, the long-established national firm Čedok offers a full range of services. Its office in central Prague is at:

Na příkopě 18, 110 00 Prague, tel: 221 447 242, fax: 224 216 324.

WEBSITES AND INTERNET RESOURCES

There are plenty of internet cafés in Prague and elsewhere, and many upmarket hotels offer internet access.

All Czech towns and cities have an official website, often with visitor information in English. Try typing <www.townname.cz> in your web browser, or simply enter the name of the town on a search engine.

Other useful websites include:

<www.czech.cz> Basic information on the country from the Czech Foreign Ministry.

<www.czechtourism.com> Czech Tourism's site, which gives general travel information.

<www.jizdnirad.cz> Comprehensive public transport information.

<www.mapy.cz> Maps and plans.

<www.myczechrepublic.com> Useful general facts and advice.

<www.pis.cz> Comprehensive information on Prague from the city's tourist information service.

<www.praguepost.cz> News and listings from the weekly English-language newspaper.

YOUTH HOSTELS

Conventional youth hostels are few and far between in the Czech Republic, but the cheaper kind of hotel may well turn out to be within the budget traveller's resources. There are backpackers' hostels of variable quality in the cities, but probably the best option for young travellers looking for really inexpensive accommodation is the *kolej*, the student hostel vacated by its normal residents during university holidays (June to August). These are to be found in every place with higher education establishments, and information about them can be obtained from local tourist information centres. Don't expect great comfort. Other hostels, called *ubytovna*, are mostly geared to the needs of migrant workers and are best avoided.

Recommended Hotels

The following list of places to stay includes hotels in most of the cities and regions described in this guide, among them modest lodgings as well as luxury establishments. Advance booking is usually unnecessary except in high season and in Prague, where there is pressure on accommodation throughout the year. Note also that prices are considerably higher in Prague than elsewhere, though in almost every case there will be special offers worth investigating.

As a basic guide to prices (given in euros) for a double room with breakfast we have used the following symbols:

€€€€€	over €250
€€€€	€150–250
€€€	€100–150
€€	€70–100
€	below €70

PRAGUE

Adria €€€€ *Václavské náměstí 26, Prague 1, tel: 221 081 111,* <www.adria.cz>. A family-owned luxury hotel in an extremely convenient position at the lower end of Wenceslas Square. The exterior is rococo in style, the interior contemporary. The rooms at the back of the hotel overlook the green oasis of the Franciscan Garden.

Aria €€€€€ *Tržiště 9, Malá Strana, Prague 1, tel: 225 334 111,* <www.aria.cz>. This establishment, in the same Malá Strana street as the US Embassy, offers superlative comfort, as well as an ingenious and fascinating musical theme pervading all aspects of its design.

Four Seasons €€€€€ *Veleslavínova 2a, Staré Město, Prague 1, tel: 221 427 000,* <www.fourseasons.com/prague>. Occupying a trio of immaculately converted historic buildings a few paces from

Charles Bridge, and offering incomparable river views, the Four Seasons is a noble addition to the city's range of top hotels.

Ibis Praha Old Town €€€ *Na Poříčí 7, Nové Město, Prague 1, tel: 221 800 800, <www.accorhotels.com>*. The Ibis chain has several hotels in Prague, of which this is the most attractive. It is also the best- located; billed as being in Old Town, it is in fact in the northern extension of the New Town, but nevertheless within a stone's throw of the Municipal House and a short walk to Old Town Square.

K&K Central €€€€€ *Hybernská 10, Nové Město, Prague 1, tel: 225 022 000, <www.kkhotels.com>*. One of Prague's loveliest Art Nouveau buildings has been reconstructed with the utmost sensitivity to provide a sumptuous environment for discriminating guests, a few minutes' walk from the Municipal House and the Old Town.

Luník €€€ *Londýnská 50, Vinohrady, Prague-Vinohrady, tel: 224 253 974, <www.hotel-lunik.cz>*. This family hotel in the inner suburb of Vinohrady is a short walk from the upper end of Wenceslas Square and even nearer to a Metro station. An attractive budget option.

Mandarin Oriental €€€€€ *Nebovidská 1, Malá Strana, Prague 1, tel: 233 088 888, <www.mandarinoriental.com>*. A 14th-century monastery in the tranquil heart of Malá Strana has metamorphosed into a supremely tasteful, contemporary hotel. Includes a spa.

U Zlaté studně €€€€ *U Zlaté studně 166/4, Malá Strana, Prague 1, tel: 257 011 213, <www.zlatastudna.cz>*. At the top of a cobbled lane, and almost clinging to the castle walls, the 'Golden Well' is a converted historic building overlooking the rooftops of Malá Strana.

SOUTHERN BOHEMIA

ČESKÉ BUDĚJOVICE

Grand Hotel Zvon €–€€€ *Náměstí Přemysla Otakara II 28, 370 01 České Budějovice, tel: 381 601 601, <www.hotel-zvon.cz>*. Rich in historical associations, the renovated 'Bell' stands on Budějovice's incomparable main square. Comfortable rooms, particularly in the five-star-rated 'Executive' category. Gourment restaurant.

Malý pivovar €€ *Karla IV 8-10, 370 01 České Budějovice, tel: 386 360 471, <www.malypivovar.cz>.* Historic arcaded building just a step from the main square, with a limited number of attractively furnished, comfortable rooms. Its Budvarka pub is one of the best places to down a few glasses of famous Budvar beer.

ČESKÝ KRUMLOV

Hotel na Louži € *Kájovská 66, 381 01 Český Krumlov, tel: 380 771 280, <www.nalouzi.cz>.* A perfectly acceptable budget alternative to the expensive Růže *(see below)*, this little establishment in the middle of medieval Krumlov has 11 very individual rooms with showers. It also has a pub serving solid Czech fare.

Růže €€€€ *Horní 154, 381 01 Český Krumlov, tel: 380 772 100, <www.hotelruze.cz>.* The supremely luxurious 'Rose' occupies Krumlov's old Jesuit college, and offers every comfort in an authentically historic ambience.

JINDŘICHŮV HRADEC

Bílá paní € *Dobrovského 5, 377 01 Jindřichův Hradec, tel: 384 362 660, <www.hotelbilapani.cz>.* A tiny, well-kept hotel in a fascinating old town house in the centre of this historic southern Bohemian town. With showers, the rooms are pleasantly furnished in contemporary style, making this a very attractive budget option. In addition there is a characterful restaurant.

TŘEBOŇ

Zlatá Hvězda €€ *Masarykovo náměstí 107, 379 01 Třeboň, tel: 333 757 111, <www.zhvezda.cz>.* On Třeboň's charming square, this fine Renaissance edifice is the best place to stay in town. Třeboň is a spa town, and hotel guests have access to the facilities at the nearby Berta Spa.

WESTERN BOHEMIA

CHEB

Zámek Mostov €€ *Mostov 1, 350 02 Cheb, tel: 354 597 277, <www.mostov.cz>*. Just off the main road linking Cheb with Karlovy Vary, this mock-Gothic castle is a useful stopping-off point for motorists arriving in the country from Germany. Considerable comfort and lots of atmosphere, plus an excellent restaurant.

FRANTIŠKOVY LÁZNĚ (FRANZENSBAD)

Kamenný Dům € *Ruská 6, 351 01 Františkovy Lázně, tel: 354 541 037, <www.kamennydum.cz>*. Founded originally as the 'Steinhaus' in 1812, this little hotel offers attractive rooms and a variety of treatments. You may be asked to take the full-board option.

Tři Lilie €€ *Národní 10, 351 01 Františkovy Lázně, tel: 354 208 900, <www.franzensbad.cz>*. This 200-year-old, modest-sized establishment has been immaculately refurbished and is probably the best place to stay in the region. Discreet luxury combined with a family atmosphere, a central location, spa treatments and a gastronomic restaurant.

KARLOVY VARY (CARLSBAD)

Čajkovskij €€€ *Sadová 44–46, 360 01 Karlovy Vary, tel: 353 237 520, <www.cajkovskij.com>*. This recently converted building is now an intimate four-star hotel, offering a high standard of comfort and facilities including full spa treatments.

Embassy €€ *Nová louka 21, 360 01 Karlovy Vary, tel: 353 221 161, <www.embassy.cz>*. Cosy, family-run four-star hotel in a historic building of great charm, along with one of the town's best restaurants.

Grand Hotel Pupp €€€€ *Mírové náměstí 2, 360 91 Karlovy Vary, tel: 353 221 161, <www.pupp.cz>*. This is the five-star, great-grandmother of all spa hotels, founded in the 18th century and patronised by the world's rich and famous ever since. It incorporates the four-star Park Hotel Pupp, only slightly less opulent. Choice of restaurants, cafés and bars. Check for seasonal specials.

LOKET

Bílý kůň € *T. G. Masaryka 109, 357 33 Loket nad Ohří, tel: 353 685 002.* The famous old 'White Horse' on the curving main square was where the elderly Goethe consorted with his teenage love Ulrike von Lewetzow. The building has been refurbished and offers reasonably priced accommodation in this delightful little medieval town.

MARIÁNSKÉ LÁZNĚ (MARIENBAD)

Koliba € *Dusíkova 592, 353 01 Mariánské Lázně, tel: 354 625 169, <www.koliba.xercom.cz>.* The 'Chalet' is a kind of mountain hut, prettily built in timber, in complete contrast to the stucco, wedding-cake establishments in the centre of town a few minutes' walk away. Limited number of rustically furnished, inexpensive rooms.

Nové Lázně €€€€ *Reitenbergerova 53, 353 01 Mariánské Lázně, tel: 354 644 111, <www. marienbad.cz>.* Built in 1896, this architectural extravaganza was just to the taste of Edward VII, who patronised the 'New Spa' on his visits here, and it is still *the* place to gain a sense of the town's glory days. It offers the full range of spa treatments.

Villa Butterfly €€€ *Hlavní 655, 353 01 Mariánské Lázně, tel: 354 654 111, <www.marienbad.cz>.* This large hotel continues the spa tradition of opulent building, here in flamboyant postmodern style.

PLZEŇ (PILSEN)

Hotel Continental €€ *Zbojnická 8, 305 34 Plzeň, tel: 377 235 292, <www.hotelcontinental.cz>.* Founded in 1895 by the Plzeň brewery and refurbished in Art Deco style in the late 1920s, this extremely grand, centrally located establishment briefly became the US Army's HQ in western Czechoslovakia in 1945. Its rooms, some of them themed, are steadily being refurbished.

TEPLÁ

Hotel Klášter Teplá € *Klášter Teplá 10, 364 61 Teplá, tel: 353 392 264, <www.hotelklastertepla.cz>*. The monks of Teplá have converted some of the monastery's substantial outbuildings into a very serviceable, medium-sized hotel, whose rooms reflect contemporary standards of comfort rather than monkish austerity.

NORTH AND EAST BOHEMIA

DĚČÍN

Hotel Česká Koruna € *Masarykovo náměstí 60, 405 01 Děčín, tel: 412 516 104, <www.hotelceskakoruna.cz>*. The 'Czech Crown' offers attractive and comfortable modern rooms in the centre of this town on the River Elbe close to the Bohemian Switzerland National Park. Its restaurant serves refined Czech and international cuisine.

HŘENSKO

Praha €€ *407 17 Hřensko, tel: 412 554 006, <www.hotel-hrensko. cz>*. Hřensko's best hotel lies a short distance upstream on the banks of the little River Kamenice, well away from the souvenir stands clustered along the main road running along the River Labe. It also has a recommendable restaurant.

LITOMYŠL

Zlatá hvězda €–€€ *Smetanovo náměstí 84, 570 01 Litomyšl, tel: 461 615 338, <www.zlatahvezda.com>*. A distinguished building on the main square of Litomyšl, the attractively restored 'Golden Star' was the natural choice when seven Central European presidents staged a summit here in 1994.

PARDUBICE

Zlatá Štika € *Štrossova 127, 530 03 Pardubice, tel: 466 052 100, <www.zlatastika.cz>*. Friendly, family-run establishment, a short walk from the historic centre of Pardubice on the far bank of the River Elbe. Attractive interior featuring works of art, comfortably furnished rooms, refined dining, pub and wine cellar.

ŠPINDLERŮV MLÝN

Harmony Club Hotel € *Bedřichov 106, 543 51 Špindlerův Mlýn, tel: 499 469 111, <www.harmonyclub.cz>*. Showing signs that its design originated in Communist times, this large hotel in a beautiful setting is nevertheless one of the best options in the Krkonoše, fully brought up to date in 2005 and with a good range of facilities.

Hotel Praha €€€ *Okruzní 118, 543 51 Špindlerův Mlýn, tel: 499 523 516, <www.spindl-hotelpraha.cz>*. Century-old edifice attractively restored, with comfortable rooms enjoying views of the mountains and the centre of this highland resort. Probably the most attractive place to stay in the area. Restaurant and summer terrace.

NORTHERN MORAVIA

BESKYDY MOUNTAINS

Hotel Tanečnica € *Pustevny, 756 57 Horní Bečva, tel: 556 835 341, <www.tanecnica.cz>*. In 1926, the architect Dušan Jurkovič built this superb chalet in the mountain resort of Pustevny, at the end of the highest road in the range. Straightforward, inexpensive lodgings.

OLOMOUC

Arigone € *Univerzitní 20, 771 00 Olomouc, tel: 585 232 351, <www.arigone.cz>*. Historic building in the university quarter with exposed stonework and heavy timber ceilings. Inexpensive restaurant.

Gemo €€–€€€ *Pavelčákova 22, 772 00 Olomouc, tel: 585 232 115, <www.hotel-gemo.cz>*. With a severely modern exterior, what was once a medieval town mansion has contemporary rooms of considerable refinement. Central location just a few steps from Olomouc's main square.

OSTRAVA

Imperial €€–€€€ *Tyršova 6, 701 38 Ostrava, tel: 599 099 717,
<www.imperial.cz>*. Century-old rebuilt grand hotel in the city
centre with all amenities, including a saltwater pool and a choice of
places to eat, among them a gourmet restaurant and brasserie.

SOUTHERN MORAVIA

BRNO

Grand Hotel €€€ *Benešova 18-20, 657 83 Brno, tel: 542 518
262, <www.grandhotelbrno.cz>*. A large neoclassical edifice dating
from 1870, located in the historical centre just a short distance from
the railway station, the Grand Hotel is a city institution offering all
comforts and facilities, including sauna and casino.

Royal Ricc €€€ *Starobrněnská 10, 602 00 Brno, tel: 542 219
262, <www.romantichotels.cz>*. A little Baroque palace in the city
centre has been made into the most charming, if not the cheapest
place to stay in Brno. Original features have been retained and enhanced, adding distinction to comfort. Restaurant with French and
Italian cuisine.

KROMĚŘÍŽ

Excellent € *Riegrovo náměstí 163/7, 767 01 Kroměříž, tel:573
333 023, <www.excellent.tunker.com>*. Superior pension on a
square in the Old Town of Kroměříž, with comfortable rooms, wine
cellar, sauna and internet access.

ZLÍN

Hotel Moskva € *Náměstí Práce 2512, 762 70 Zlín, tel: 577 561
111, <www.moskva-zlin.cz>*. When spending a night in Tomáš
Bat'a's shoe metropolis, it makes sense to check into one of the
town's iconic buildings, this 10-storey 'skyscraper' of 1930, which
has all the facilities of a grand hotel at a modest price.

LEDNICE–VALTICE AREA

Hraniční zámeček € *Hlohovec u Břeclaví 16, tel: 519 354 353/4,
<www.hranicnizamecek.cz>*. Built by the Liechtensteins in 1819 and
attractively converted into a characterful hotel, the 'Border Castle' is
an ideal place to stay for those wanting to absorb more of the atmosphere of the parklands between the castles at Lednice and Valtice.

LUHAČOVICE

Jurkovíčův dům €€ *Lázenskňe námestí 109, 763 26 Luhačovice,
tel: 577 129 111, <www.lazneluhacovice.cz/jurkovic>*. A four-star
hotel completely renovated in 2002, this is the most flamboyant of
all the buildings designed by Art Nouveau architect Dušan Jurkovič.

MIKULOV

Rohatý krokodýl € *Husova 8, 692 01 Mikulov, tel: 519 510
692, <www.rohatykrokodyl.cz>*. In the former ghetto, the 'Horned
Crocodile' is the most attractive place to stay in this wine town.
Limited number of pleasantly furnished rooms, plus restaurant,
pub and artworks throughout.

TELČ

Černý orel € *Náměstí Zachariáše z Hradec 7, 588 56 Telč, tel:
567 243 222. <www.hotelcernyorel.cz>*. The largest hotel in this
utterly charming little town has an unbeatable location on the main
square as well as good standard accommodation. In a historic 16th-
century building, it also has a restaurant and garden terrace.

ZNOJMO

Hotel Prestige €€ *Pražská 100, 669 02 Znojmo, tel: 515 224 595,
<www.hotel-prestige.cz>*. In a suburban location and targeted at
business travellers, the old 'Friendship Hotel' has been completely
overhauled, and offers comfortable, four-star rooms with contemporary furnishings as well as a wide range of facilities.

Recommended Restaurants

It is difficult to go hungry when travelling around the Czech Republic. There are basic restaurants to be found virtually everywhere, though you may have to look hard in order to get away from the standard fare of pork, cabbage and dumplings. Some of the best restaurants are those attached to hotels, particularly those with a four-star grading. Many such establishments are listed in the previous section, and you should refer to this as well as to the recommendations below. A small number of exceptionally interesting or attractive cafés are listed as well. Eating out is rarely expensive, except in Prague where a number of restaurants catering mostly to foreigners are able to charge international prices.

The symbols below give some idea of the average cost (in Czech crowns) of a meal for one, excluding drinks:

€€€€	over Kč1,000
€€€	Kč500–1,000
€€	Kč300–500
€	below Kč300

PRAGUE

Celnice €–€€ *V Celnici 4, Nové Město, tel: 224 212 240.* The Kolkovna Group (owned by Pilsner Urquell) has opened a number of highly contemporary 'super-pubs' in Prague, of which this, the 'Customs House', is one. It serves satisfying Czech fare in a stylish ambience for very reasonable prices, especially if you order the daily special.

David €€€ *Tržiště 21, Malá Strana, tel: 257 533 109.* Tucked away on a cobblestoned street in Malá Strana, this refined little two-room establishment greets its customers like private guests, and treats them to temptingly refined versions of traditional Czech dishes.

Hergetova Cihelna €€€–€€€€ *Cihelná 2b, Malá Strana, tel: 257 535 534.* Trendy restaurant in a converted brickworks on the banks of the Vltava. Spacious bar, and dining room with riverside terrace.

Nebozízek €€€ *Petřínské sady 411, Malá Strana, tel: 257 315 329.* Set in greenery, and reached from the halfway station on the Petřín Hill funicular, this is one of the most attractive of Prague's panoramic restaurants, and the food is quite acceptable, too.

Obecní dům €€–€€€€ *Náměstí Republiky 5, Staré Město, tel: 222 002 770.* The resplendent Art Nouveau Municipal House has three places to eat: a glittering French restaurant, a beer cellar with traditional hearty offerings, and a gorgeous café.

U Pinkasů €–€€ *Jungmannovo náměstí 16, Nové Město, tel: 221 11 150.* Downstairs there's a pub, while upstairs you can dine in a more relaxed atmosphere. The roast duck is delicious.

CENTRAL BOHEMIA

KARLŠTEJN

Romantic Hotel Mlýn €€ *Karlštejn 101, tel: 311 744 411.* There are plenty of eating options by Karlštejn Castle or in the nearby village, but it's worth taking the short walk along the River Berounka to this restaurant, in an old mill. Fish specialities. Closed Mon–Tues.

KONOPIŠTĚ

Stará myslivna €€ *Konopiště 2, tel: 317 721 148.* The spirit of Habsburg huntsman Franz Ferdinand pervades this establishment in the forest close to his castle, where a medley of hunting trophies sets the tone for dishes based on boar, pheasant, partridge and venison.

KŘIVOKLÁT

U Jelena €€ *Hradní 53, tel: 313 558 529.* Hunting-themed restaurant serving game specialities, among other Czech offerings.

KUTNÁ HORA

Pivnice Dačický €€ *Rakova 8, tel: 327 512 248.* This is a cheerful medieval-themed beer hall in the centre of town dishing up traditional Czech food, washed down with a choice of draught beers.

LITOMĚŘICE

Salva Guarda €€ *Mírové náměstí 12, tel: 416 732 506.* This striking building on Litoměřice's main square is now a hotel. Beneath the Gothic vaults of the ground floor, a restaurant serves Bohemian specialities, notably game, accompanied by local wines.

MĚLNÍK

Zámecká restaurace €–€€ *Svatováclavská 19, tel: 315 622 121.* Despite getting very busy during the season, Mělník's Castle Restaurant is as good a place as any to eat in this little town, not least because of its list of local wines and its terrace overlooking the confluence of the rivers Vltava and Elbe.

PRŮHONICE

Hliněná bašta €€ *Újezdská 619, tel: 272 690 700.* Almost within sight of Prague, the village of Průhonice with its castle offers visitors a taste of the Bohemian countryside. As does this fascinating establishment, the 'Earthen Bastion', built from old materials and incorporating all kinds of sustainable technology. The food is good as well!

SOUTHERN BOHEMIA

ČESKÉ BUDĚJOVICE

Alchymista €€ *U tří lvů 10, tel: 386 356 545.* Deep in its brick-vaulted cellar, the 'Alchemist' boasts a lineage going back to the time of Emperor Rudolf II and his retinue of quacks and soothsayers. A number of themed specialities ('The Philosopher's Stone', 'Executioner's Special') are prepared in an 'alchemist's oven'.

ČESKÝ KRUMLOV

Krčma v Šatlavské ulici €€ *Horní 157, tel: 380 713 344.* The ancient 'Tavern in Lock-up Street' delivers the full medieval Monty, with songs and swordfights and general revelry to accompany roast sucking pig from the spit and similar offerings.

The Old Inn €€€ *Náměstí Svornost 12, tel: 380 772 500.* On the town's main square, the Old Inn is a comfortable hotel with a good restaurant, beer cellar with charcoal grill, pub and outdoor terrace.

JINDŘICHŮV HRADEC

Golden Goose €€€ *Náměstí Míru 141, tel: 384 362 320.* The Golden Goose is the main restaurant of what is the best hotel in this lovely south Bohemian town, with fresh fish from the local carp ponds as one of its specialities. Alternatively, there's a Chinese eatery and a pub.

ŠUMAVA

Šumava Inn €€ *Kvilda 22, tel: 388 405 511.* In the heart of the national park, Kvilda is the highest village in the Czech Republic. Previously called 'The King of the Šumava', this chalet-style guesthouse offers hearty traditional food in its restaurant.

TŘEBOŇ

Šupina €–€€ *Valy, tel: 384 721 149.* The 'Fish Scale', with its outdoor terrace, is probably the best place to try local specialities harvested from the fish ponds of this part of southern Bohemia.

WESTERN BOHEMIA

KARLOVY VARY (CARLSBAD)

Promenáda €€€ *Tržiště 31, tel: 353 225 648.* The gourmet restaurant of this family-run hotel serves up original cuisine with an international touch in a cosy atmosphere. Good selection of wines.

Vinárna Karla IV €€ *Zámecký vrch 2, tel: 353 227 255*. Occupying a 17th-century building, this restaurant has plenty of atmosphere to accompany its wide range of satisfying dishes.

Zámecký vrch €€€ *Zámecký vrch 14, tel: 353 221 321*. Intimate establishment specialising in sophisticated Bohemian cuisine.

MARIÁNSKÉ LÁZNĚ (MARIENBAD)

Kladská Pension €€€ *Kladská 6, tel: 354 691 888*. Deep in the forest 10km (6 miles) north of Mariánské Lázně, this chalet guesthouse has a fine restaurant featuring a number of well-chosen specialities.

U Zlaté koule €€€–€€€€ *Nehrova 26, tel: 354 624 455*. This opulent establishment offers game from the surrounding forests and many choice dishes besides, along with an extensive list of Moravian and international wines. Two days' notice is required for the most toothsome speciality, goose with a liver stuffing.

PLZEŇ (PILSEN)

U Mansfelda €–€€ *Dřevěná 9, tel: 377 333 844*. One of Plzeň's more refined establishments, offering wine as well as beer to go with its above-average selection of traditional Czech dishes.

U Salzmannů €–€€ *Pražská 8, tel: 377 235 855*. This wood-panelled city institution claims to be the oldest beer hall in Plzeň, and it certainly delivers the goods, with solid Bohemian fare (duck, rabbit, pork knuckle), washed down with lashings of Pilsener.

TEPLÁ

Klášter Teplá €–€€ *Klášter Teplá 10, 364 61 Teplá, tel: 353 392 264*. The restaurant of Teplá monastery is one of the more interesting places to eat in the 'West Bohemian Triangle', with run-of-the-mill Czech food supplemented by specialities which can be ordered in advance, among them ominous-sounding 'Pferdeäpfel' (German for horse droppings). There's also a pub serving Pilsener.

NORTH AND EAST BOHEMIA

DĚČÍN

Paštýřská stěna € *Žižkova 236/6, tel: 412 532 198.* One of the sights of Děčín is the sheer cliff – the 'Shepherd's Wall' – rising high above the Elbe on the far bank of the river. The climb is worth it not only for the view but also for this restaurant with reliable Bohemian cooking.

HRADEC KRÁLOVÉ

Nové Albertinum € *Velké náměstí 32, tel: 495 063 111.* Located on the main square, the city's old Jesuit college now houses a restaurant offering well-prepared Czech dishes at very reasonable prices.

LIBEREC

Ambiente € *Sokolská 1365, tel: 485 108 815.* The local branch of a trendy Prague establishment with a wide range of Italian, Mexican and Texan dishes.

Kavárna Pošta *Náměstí E Beneše 24, tel: 485 110 021.* Sumptuous Viennese-style café strategically placed to welcome theatre-goers. Worth a visit for its own sake, as well as for the usual café offerings.

LITOMYŠL

Pod klášterem € *Boženy Němcové 158, tel: 461 615 901.* This pension-restaurant serves Czech and international dishes in its brick-vaulted basement as well as on the ground floor. The food can be enhanced by choosing a Moravian wine from the extensive wine list.

NOVÉ MĚSTO NAD METUJÍ

Peklo € *Jestřebí 30, tel: 491 422 615.* Idyllically located outside the town, this fanciful timber structure was built as a summer retreat for the Bartoň family, owners of the castle in Nové Město, and is now a characterful restaurant.

NORTHERN MORAVIA

OLOMOUC

Moravská restaurace €€ *Horní náměstí 23, tel 585 222 868.* Centrally located establishment with a traditional theme. Costumed staff serve local specialities just like their Moravian mothers made them.

OSTRAVA

Moravská chalupa €€ *Musorgského 9, tel: 596 124 937.* In the middle of the city, this rustic establishment recreates the atmosphere of the Moravian countryside with large servings of 'peasant' food.

SOUTHERN MORAVIA

BRNO

U Královny Elišky €€ *Mendlovo náměstí 1a, tel: 543 212 578.* The Augustinians' wine cellars have been converted into a rustic dining experience featuring Moravian dishes and music to match.

Ristorante Rialto €€€ *Veveří 125, 616 00 Brno, tel: 541 235 035.* Stylish establishment in an easy-to-reach location north of the centre. Italian and international specialities with a contemporary touch.

KROMĚŘÍŽ

Holub €€ *Kollárova 5, tel: 573 339 342.* This opulent villa houses a four-star pension as well as a restaurant reckoned to be the best in town. Czech and international dishes.

LEDNICE–VALTICE AREA

Valtická rychta €€ *Mikulovská 165, Valtice, tel: 519 352 366.* Prettily renovated traditional village house with a folksy interior and good food to match, including 'delicate roast knee' – that is, succulent pork knuckle. Well-stocked wine cellar.

INDEX